Advocates
P. O. Box 155
Hot Sulphur Springs, CO 80451-0155

Who
Is
Angela Davis?

Who
Is
Angela Davis?

The Biography of
a Revolutionary

by

Regina Nadelson

Peter H. Wyden, Inc. / Publisher
New York

WHO *IS* ANGELA DAVIS?

LIBRARY OF CONGRESS CATALOG CARD NUMBER: 72–85993

MANUFACTURED IN THE UNITED STATES OF AMERICA

For my mother and father with much love.

Acknowledgment

I would like to thank everyone who helped me with this book. There are too many to mention each by name, but a few demand special thanks and gratitude: Henry McGee of the University of California in Los Angeles who has been from the very beginning wonderfully, endlessly generous with his time and knowledge; Maureen McConville of Patrick Seale and Associates who made the actual writing of this book rewarding when it would otherwise have been an overwhelming chore; Mrs. Sallye Davis and Mr. Frank Davis who were not only kind and helpful, but made my visit to Birmingham a unique and wonderful experience; and above all Angela who gave of her time even while withstanding the terrible months in prison.

I also want to thank all the friends and relatives here and abroad who put me up and put up with me, especially and always Anne Graham Bell.

Contents

Prologue: Notes on a Journey   xi

Part I: **THE SELLING OF A SYMBOL**   1

Part II: **THE SOUTH: GROWING UP**   15
   1. Bombingham, Alabama   17
   2. Growing Up American   25
   3. Out of a Tradition   38

Part III: **GOING NORTH**   49
   4. At Home in Brooklyn   51
   5. High School and Picket Lines   57
   6. Brandeis: A Liberal Education   73
   7. An American in Paris   85

Part IV: **A RADICAL PROCESS**   95
   8. Senior Year: A Meeting with Marcuse   97
   9. Germany: Philosophy and Politics   104
   10. California, USA   120
   11. A Political Commitment: the Che Lumumba Club   131

Part V: **THE MAKING OF A CAUSE**   139
   12. Red Tape   141
   13. On Campus, For Credit, As Planned   153
   14. Spring 1970: The Firing of Angela Davis   165

Part VI: **SAN RAFAEL AND AFTER**   177
   15. August 7   179
   16. Conversations in Jail   189
   17. The People vs. The State of California   195

Epilogue: More Notes on a Journey   199

Index   201

PROLOGUE: NOTES ON A JOURNEY

In the early summer of 1969 an anthropology student at the University of California at Los Angeles wrote an article for the student newspaper. In it he asserted that a new member of the Department of Philosophy was a member of the Communist Party. The student was a paid informer for the FBI, a fact not revealed until months later. Nobody took much notice of him until July 9, when a reporter on the *San Francisco Examiner* picked up the story and published an article revealing the name of the young philosopher. The Regents of the University of California sent her a letter demanding to know whether she was in fact a Communist. Yes, she said, avowing her affiliation in an open letter. On September 19, 1969, she was fired. The young woman's name was Angela Davis.

When the Regents fired Angela Davis, they lit a fuse that was to burn for months. Fired in September, reinstated by the courts to her job soon after, she continued to teach in an atmosphere of increasing conflict until, in June of 1970, she was finally dismissed for "inflammatory speeches" in defense of the Soledad Brothers, the three black convicts accused of killing a white prison guard the previous January.

By June interest in her case had died down. The media went away, the glamour wore off, school closed for the summer. The fire, it seemed, had gone out. But Angela Davis' case was still in the courts, and few realized something the Regents knew: she stood a good chance to win. In August the bomb exploded.

On August 7, 1970, a young man named Jonathan Jackson walked into a courtroom at San Rafael, California. Armed with guns, he freed three black convicts present in court. Taking the judge and several others for hostages, Jackson tried to escape in a van parked outside the courthouse. There was gunfire. When the incident was over, the judge, two of the convicts, and Jonathan Jackson were dead.

As a result of what happened at San Rafael two people were charged with kidnapping, murder, and conspiracy. One was Ruchell Magee, the only convict present in court on August 7 left alive. The other was twenty-six-year-old Angela Davis.

Under California law anyone providing weapons with the *intent* that they be used for the crime committed is as guilty as those who pull the triggers. The guns that Jonathan Jackson carried into court that day were alleged to have been purchased by Angela Davis. In October 1970 she was imprisoned and, after a trial in the spring of 1972, acquitted of all charges.

Those are the barest facts of the two incidents that have made Angela Davis a public figure. Had they not happened, she would eventually have made her mark. These incidents apart, she would inevitably have been—as I believe she will be again—important in a public context. But she would not be an international name today and no one would yet have written about her. However, at the same time as the events at UCLA and San Rafael thrust her into prominence, they spawned instant interpreters by the dozen to submerge her in legal and sociological jargon, garishly colored by the sensationalism that began the moment she was fired.

This book is an attempt to dig beneath the distorting columns of newsprint and discover who Angela Davis, in all her personal and political complexity, really is. About the case itself I am not going to say much, but I want to put on record that everything I know of Angela made me believe her from the start—long before the courts affirmed my belief by acquitting her—when she said, "I am innocent of all charges." And obviously my attitude informs what I write. Some will then question my competence to write this book. Some will also question my capacity as a white person to do so. I make no defense. But I also try to make no assumptions. I cannot pretend that I have met and seen and talked with everyone Angela has known. Many of her friends, especially those she knew in California, were busy working on her defense by the time I got to them. But I tried to set down all I have learned—from reading, from Angela, from her friends, her family, her colleagues. For if Angela is not seen as a real person, but is just passed over as a case or a cause, how much easier to pass over the thousands of others who are not even recognized as causes, much less as human beings.

My journey in search of Angela Davis began when I couldn't even know it was beginning or that it was to be a journey. A journey that would take me through America and into my own past as well as hers. Perhaps it began when my mother handed me the clipping and said, "Remember Angie Davis?" It was September of 1969. I had come home from England, en route to California. I looked through the article, which stated that Angela Davis, a member of the Communist Party, had been fired from her teaching job at UCLA. I followed the news reports carefully, but the young woman in the headlines barely resembled the girl I'd known in high school. Of course, that was a decade ago; we weren't close enough to have kept up.

Maybe, though, it all came about because we are the same age and grew up in the same America, and followed, initially, not dissimilar paths. I knew Angela first when we were just old enough to reach out and look at and deal with the world—in an immediate way and with all the inconsistencies of sixteen. She was the first black person I knew well enough to ask, "What's it really like?"

I met her again in California in 1970, when she was trying to change the world. What impressed me then was her strength, her patience, and a kind of toughness that allowed her to cope with a reality she willingly recognized. She had no need of illusions. There was a confidence that commitment had given her. There was also a shy gentleness and a wry good humor. And a certain inner dignity with which she faced a lot of anger and hate.

What is intriguing about her is a peculiar and rare ability to get herself across to all kinds of people—the way she meets the world in human terms. I've been across America now, to Germany and to France, and I've talked to people, dozens of them. Few deny she is in touch. Even before she knew her own direction most people felt pretty much that, as one friend put it, "Angela could walk into the tavern on the corner with the fellows and relate to them and not be condescending, and then sit around with a bunch of philosophers and relate to them. The change in terminology and almost everything else was nearly imperceptible. There was no special language. Angela's Angela everywhere. And for some reason people understand Angela wherever she's at."

This book, then, is an investigation rather than a critical analysis. Plenty of historians and sociologists and philosophers can (and doubtless will) theorize about Angela and Marxism and Communism and racism. The journalists have already made and will again make her a sensation or a symbol. I leave the maze of legal details to the experts. Nor is this a book defined by journalistic time—the limits of "news"—for that changes as rapidly as words are typed and is contrary to my very purpose to discover Angela beneath, apart from, in spite of, the events that have happened. For though it is the events that have made her public, she is worth a book anyway. The events need only be catalogued, analyzed, and dated. Angela is part of them and they are essential. But the person is apart from them—is, or else would be so light a thing, so passing and fragile as to be not more than a creation of those events, filed and forgotten with them. An interesting phenomenon, but without mind or gut. That is why this book begins by detailing the way the news media have displayed Angela. What follows is an effort to knock out the tidy clichés.

This book tries to tell about Angela as she is, as she sees herself, as her family and friends know and see her. It is about growing up black in the segregated world of Birmingham and about the complex reactions of a young girl to that world. It is about her mother and father, her brothers and her sister—a tight-knit family that protected and isolated her from the world outside and yet gave her the skills to cope with it. It is about the Southern tradition of "Help the Race" in which socialists played an important part—a tradition to which Angela belongs. It tries to tell what it is like to be Angela Davis at twenty and in Paris and about how it feels to be Angela at twenty-seven and in jail. It is about success American-style and the rejection of it. Adolescent rebellion plays a role, as does adult revolution. It is about growing up into a political being with strong ideas and a firm commitment to them, and it is about discovering an identity with one's people.

Over and over again the question has been asked, "Where did she go wrong?" She is seen as a person who suddenly pulled radical ideas from the air, turned against her middle-class upbringing, and plunged headlong into revolution. Those who pose this question ignore the traditions behind her, the life she has led. Angela does, in a sense, fit into two very different groups, and it is perhaps this dual belonging that gives her the understanding and the strength she has acquired. For, as Rudi Dutschke has claimed, "the challenge to the established order of capitalist civilization originates at the moment in two markedly different sectors of the world population: *the underclass of the colonized peoples (including American blacks) and the middle-class youth of the mother country.*

My journey has taken me to places Angela has been, to meet the people she has known. What strikes me now is her ability to grow, to perceive clearly the world around her and to change in accordance with that perception. She has proved to have the guts at least to try to reach out, to try for something she sees as better and necessary—for herself and for others.

People puzzle over her seeming ambiguity, they call her enigmatic. They are puzzled because they want to see her as a riddle—a problem with an answer, a subject to sum up in a phrase. They don't see that she is unique and that she is also like a lot of other people. She is not a tidy sum of all the parts. She is all the parts of her life, her ideas, her environment, her perceptions and emotions, the people who touched her and whom she touched. A part—the largest part—remains unknown, and that is the future. Because Angela is, I am sure, someone who is going to go on living, seeing, changing, a person who will be in the world according to the way she must.

Perhaps other books will begin where this one ends. Because of this, and because Angela is still growing, changing, my journey by its very nature must be incomplete.

PART I/THE SELLING
OF A SYMBOL

> "The day of the dirty commie Jew bastard has passed to the day of the dirty commie nigger bastard now that the black is powerful enough to be a threat."
>
> —JOEL KOVEL

On September 19, 1969, when Angela Davis was fired from her job at UCLA, she lost forever the option of being "just Angela." As the object of the sensation-makers, she was fixed in the highly visible state of fame. Her politics, her race, her intelligence, and her looks provided prime pickings for the press. She became a symbol. Would she have made history in her own good time? No doubt she would, but before she had a chance to make her mark in her own way she was coopted by the news media.

By spring of 1970 Angela had become a celebrity. It was a role she disliked intensely. Suddenly everyone wanted a piece of the goods. Reporters clamored for news and interviews. All kinds of people wanted her on television. She rejected many offers because she considered them opportunistic. A lack of interest in power or fame, a strong distaste for publicity—as much political as personal—made her withdraw from the spotlight whenever possible. On the other hand, she forced herself to meet the press and public because, as she told me, "One thing I have to do is be involved in the struggle whenever necessary. I don't consider myself a celebrity and I'm surprised when people recognize me. I just sort of block that part of it out of my mind." That was in 1970. It was going to be increasingly hard for her to do.

3

The media do not comment on history or events in the 1970s. They make them. An elapsed-time effect is achieved, speeding the object to the center of the public eye. That's what happened to Angela as she became the target of analysis, sensation, hate, and adoration, the "Black Devil" theme cropping up to alternate with the "Red Madonna" interpretation. The ingredients for one recipe or another were all there and they were tempting indeed.

Angela is young and she is articulate, she is highly intelligent. She is a black woman and she is a Communist. Good-looking, strong-minded, and totally committed, she had qualities to make the mouths of the media water with anticipation. What disturbed the press, however, was that despite a neat set of labels (black, brilliant, beautiful, red, etc., etc.), it wasn't actually all that easy to shove her into categories. Stereotypes did not suit her. If she was young, her approach to politics was cool and long-range; if she was black, she neither sucked up to the white establishment nor did she play the fanatic rhetorician. As a woman she was concerned with women's rights but never grew shrill over them. And as a Communist she never tried to "hide" the fact, nor did she "indoctrinate" others. The facts just weren't as "spicy" as they had seemed at first. Maybe the news media got mad at Angela for this and decided to add artificial flavoring.

"An Icon to New Left Activists from Coast to Coast," "Admitted Red," "Brilliant Black," the headlines screamed. It would be unfair to say that Angela was let down by the "establishment press"—that blanket under which huddle, among others, those "liberal" publications that are slightly to the left of middle. The press, in fact, took her up very much indeed. Angela stories, especially in the more liberal publications, were as popular as a Black Panther at a party in those days. And those who could not unreservedly praise

her used her as a peg for editorials in favor of academic freedom. Proving themselves liberated from fear 1950s-style,
some said clever things such as, "How could such an intelligent girl join such a reactionary organization?" (*i.e.*, the
Communist Party). And even the not notably progressive
California press grudgingly admitted that she was an excellent teacher, although in 1969 the *Los Angeles Times* did
suggest that the whole chain of events at UCLA was a plot
contrived by subversives to promote new tension between
university and students. There was also plenty of leering. I
sat in on an interview at UCLA conducted by a reporter
who had come to discuss her educational theories. This is
how it went:

REPORTER: Can I ask you a very simple question? How can I
    describe your skirt? Is it leather? Is it a brown miniskirt?
    Is it a brown leather miniskirt?
FANIA (ANGELA's *sister*): Tell him it's *cuir sauvage*.
ANGELA: No, that would be terrible.
REPORTER: Now what is that? What does that mean?
ANGELA: Well, it means wild leather—just say leather.
REPORTER: Well, is it a miniskirt? It is a miniskirt, isn't it?
ANGELA: It's a skirt. Just say a skirt, that's all.

She was asked repeatedly if her sexuality disrupted
classes. Others probed such details as why she often stood
at the lectern holding a cigarette without lighting it.

Despite reportorial efforts to sensationalize her, things
remained more or less clear cut as long as she was "wanted"
only for being a Communist. The Right Wing and much of
the local California population hated her. They were about
as keen to have a Communist in their schools as, say, a
rapist. Communism still provokes shudders of fear and hatred in much of America, and at that point California's
school system was in a state of shock from the furor over

black "radicals." Nathan Hare had been dismissed as chairman of the School of Ethnic Studies at San Francisco State College; Eldridge Cleaver had been refused permission to lecture at Berkeley. The appointment of Sydney Walton as principal of Sausalito's Martin Luther King Elementary School had produced a confrontation that made headlines; books by Eldridge Cleaver and LeRoi Jones were removed from the reading lists at San Francisco high schools. A lot of fear got mixed up in the smog that hangs low over California.

If the Right despised and feared Angela, she had become, for the Left, a heroine. From East Germany, from the Soviet Union, from the underground in scores of countries came accolades and columns of praise. In general the "establishment press," despite inaccuracies and a clever rearrangement of details in the interests of sensation, had supported Angela at UCLA. The press played it for all it was worth, and that was a great deal. Until June of 1970, when Angela was fired. By then the news was down to a dribble. Like all causes (especially those involving academic freedom), Angela had limited staying power. There were predictions that with the summer vacation she would fade into obscurity. The Regents, however, were not so offhand about her future. They knew perfectly well that she could be reinstated by the courts to her teaching job. But as soon as Angela was dismissed, on June 19, 1970, news about her dried up almost at once.

Seven weeks later the press once again found reason to interest itself in Angela Davis: she was accused of murder, kidnapping, and conspiracy in connection with the August 7 shooting at San Rafael. Here was news! And when Angela disappeared on August 15, she received the first order of publicity: the top spot on the FBI's Ten Most Wanted list. Her face appeared in every newspaper and on every television screen. She was right there, too, on the post office wall, among the bank robbers and arsonists and murderers: ". . . wanted on charges growing out of an abduction and shooting in Marin County, California, on August 7, 1970. She allegedly has purchased several guns in the past. To be considered possibly armed and dangerous." I assumed that pretty well everyone else—except the Right Wing, of course —would explode with an incredulity to match my own. It was a very naïve assumption. The "establishment press," which had supported Angela during her trials at UCLA, re-acted in a way as horrifying as Hoover's and a good deal more shocking. Most of the stories presumed her guilty, even if they put over their suspicions more subtly than the posters.

It was not for the "responsible" press to make the hos-tile assumptions of the Right-wing minor-leaguers. Instead they set out to "interpret" her, to explain her in four-color four-page cover stories. "Number one on the black militant hit parade," Eric Sevareid joked on CBS one evening, while Alistair Cooke plugged her as "The newest star on the left to replace Abbie Hoffman." The terrifying thing was that in "interpreting" Angela, the press came up with a kind of aberration in the form of a woman and, moreover, their words presumed guilt. *Life* ran a cover story called "The Making of a Fugitive" in which it was stated that a "scholar turns to hate and fanatic commitment." *Newsweek* called Angela the "most glamorous and provocative fugitive on the feds' list." Who was this girl, the press cried, who would turn down all America offered for a life of crime? How was it possible for Angela, daughter of the middle classes, edu-cated in the best establishments of America and Europe, to become a fanatic militant? Attempting to solve the puzzle she was supposed to be, the *New York Times* noted that she had "made her home at the crossroads of two cultures," and went on to explain: "Angela comes from an intellectual middle class background and that produced a tremendous internal struggle in her. . . . There was always a clash between what she wanted to do and what she felt she ought to do. She felt a great pressure to prove her revolutionary credentials, to be able to talk to the cat on the street, not just the ivory tower intellectual."

Haywood Burns, a young black lawyer who has worked on Angela's case, finds the behavior of the press objectionable on at least two counts: "No one in the media has dealt with the fact that there exists a tradition behind Angela. They have, instead, described her as if she just popped from the sea, black and beautiful from nowhere, and then went wrong. It is this concept of 'going wrong' that was so dangerous." His second point provides an insight into what prompted the public, including a great many liberals, to lose enthusiasm for Angela so fast. This unaccountably rapid reversal of feeling in effect gave credence to accusations made by California, a state rampant with demagogues like Ronald Reagan and Max Rafferty, the very state where Angela had been fired from her job. Haywood Burns offers an explanation: "Many things about Angela would attract a liberal bourgeois press. But her being linked by the government with so heinous a crime in the minds of liberals— invading the sacrosanct area of a courtroom and taking the life of a judge—predisposes them to accept the possibility of her guilt."

The photographs as much as the words influenced many. The posters everywhere and the pictures of Angela when she was caught—her hair pulled back, hands cuffed in front, the faceless federal agents holding both arms—made the simple blatant statement that here was a criminal who had been hunted and who had been caught.

In proportion as she lost support among Right-thinking Americans, so she gained it from radicals of every ideological variety. In Communist and Third World countries, as in the militant press in America, she became a symbol and a hero-ine. Many who had been divided over the question of her Party membership, or had accused her of splitting allegiances, now came together. She was in trouble at the hands of the establishment, a fact that undercut political differences. Acrobatic feats of special pleading were achieved in the efforts to account for her politics, as in a *Village Voice* article by Charles Wright: "The legend of her educational map is absurd, and on the surface has nothing to do with the thousands of blacks to whom words like revolutionary politics, capitalist, fascist, are as foreign as truffles on the moon. Freedom is their word. Yet despite her political be-liefs, Angela in her own way was fighting for the same word."

A few radical voices were out of tune with the rest. Just after her arrest William Kunstler stated in *Newsweek*, "She seems to be torn between the old line theory and her friendship with black people. Remember her education is all white oriented. Brandeis, Marcuse, the Sorbonne. The differences between the Party and the movement are irrecon-cilable. The Communist Party is against the young and their revolutionary activity. She must make a choice." In Europe extravagant articles filled the magazines. Finding her loveli-ness "immense" *L'Express* noted that even under arrest she had "the proud beauty of an exiled Queen of Sheba." And in *Der Stern* the Germans commented on the great intelli-gence "with which she mastered every field of knowledge."

The American press continued to flail about, looking for reasons to "explain" Angela's behavior. There was noth-ing in her background—no ghetto childhood, no drugs, no poverty—to which the press could assign her "bad deeds" and pardon her for them. But all of this has a lot more than semantic importance. There would be a group of men and women in a courtroom. They would hear evidence and decide Angela's fate. They all had read newspapers, had watched television, at least had seen a national magazine, if only in the dentist's waiting room. Pre-trial publicity is considered prejudicial if an assumption of guilt is created or if specific items are published concerning the crime, the arrest, or the accused. If a piece of interpretive reporting has political or racial overtones, it can be considered prejudicial. There are laws by which a judge can even declare a mistrial if he feels that pre-trial reporting has seriously influenced jurors. In the light of this tradition all that was reported about Angela really began to matter. News about the expensive security arrangements made her look very dangerous indeed. More than one story stressed the costs of the trial to local taxpayers. All of this had immediate impact on local citizens from among whom the jurors had to be selected. There were, as well, a number of insidious stories. An interesting and subtle example comes from the *New York Times*.

Two editorials appeared in the *New York Times*, one on October 9, 1969, just after Angela was fired by the Regents of the University of California, the other on October 16, 1970, just after she was arrested. The first, supporting Angela's right to teach, betrays indifference to, if not distaste for her political point of view and almost ignores her existence as an individual. The only personal observations are that the UCLA Department of Philosophy "attested to her scholarly competence" and that her "political affiliation, no matter how misguided," posed less of a threat to the university than did the Regents. The second editorial abandons consideration of principle to focus on personality, finding Angela "beautiful, brilliant and committed . . . an eloquent spokesman for radical causes," and continuing, suggests quite explicitly that she is closely linked to the events at San Rafael. These are the editorials in full:

POLITICAL TEST AT UCLA

After arrogating to themselves veto power over faculty appointments last June, the Regents of the University of California then tried to mollify the campus by vowing that "no political test shall ever be considered in the hiring and firing of teachers." Less than three months after that pledge was given, the Regents discharged Angela Davis, assistant professor of philosophy at the university's Los Angeles campus, because she is, by her own admission, a member of the American Communist Party. Miss Davis undoubtedly alarmed the increasingly conservative Reagan-dominated Regents by her militant opinions and former membership in the Students for a Democratic Society and the Black Panthers. But the philosophy department has attested to her scholarly competence; and since it is her political affiliations rather than her actions in the classroom that are being penalized, the Regents are plainly applying the "political test" they recently disavowed. To justify their action, the Regents invoked a 1940 resolution (reaffirmed in 1949) which declared Communist Party membership incompatible with service on the faculty. The UCLA Faculty Senate, aware of the political anachronism and angered by the Regents' interference, has now overwhelmingly rescinded the ban on Communists and is testing the legality of the Regents' action in the courts. Well they might because the real issue is academic freedom. Concern over this basic principle has already aroused an essentially moderate campus and is sure to play into the hands of the truly destructive forces of the revolutionary left. The public spectacle of UCLA's chancellor being ordered to do the Regents' bidding despite his firmly stated disagreement, is a blow to the independence of the entire university system. It is reminiscent of the shameful days of the early 30s when professors were threatened with dismissal for refusal to sign loyalty oaths.

The Regents' reliance on political informers on campus is equally ominous. The prospect of spying and of purges in the academic community poses a far more serious threat to the future of the university and of a free society than the political affiliation, no matter how misguided, of one professor.*

THE ANGELA DAVIS TRAGEDY

Beautiful, brilliant and committed, Angela Davis rocketed to national attention as an effective and eloquent spokesman for radical causes. At the University of California at Los Angeles, efforts by the Regents to remove her from the faculty surrounded her with an aura of martyrdom and won her wide sympathy even from many who did not agree with her politics. Then, last August, the bloody shoot-out at the courthouse in San Rafael was followed by charges that she had been an accomplice of those who invaded the judicial chambers with guns. Miss Davis dropped from sight and a national and international hunt for her began.

Now Miss Davis has been caught as the end result of what appears to have been a brilliant investigative effort by the Federal Bureau of Investigation. Already attempts are under way by her defenders to politicize her case and to deflect attention from the specifics of the charges against her to the merits of the causes she espoused. Whatever the eventual outcome, the tragedy is that one who might have made a significant contribution to the nation's normal political debate and to

* *The New York Times*, October 9, 1969.

its needed processes of peaceful change became so alienated that she finally went over to revolutionary words and perhaps worse.*

Not only did the press make Angela look very guilty; it ignored what people who knew her told it. Her friends and colleagues complained repeatedly of being misquoted or intentionally misunderstood. News about her came out, it seemed, on a conveyor belt, and many didn't bother even to sort Angela out from other women who were also black and militant. One evening San Francisco's television station WPIX broadcast a story about Angela. It was August 1971. Pre-trial hearings were in progress in San Rafael, and Bay Area newspapers were carrying daily pictures of her. As the reporter talked a photo of Kathleen Cleaver flashed on the screen. Someone had obviously pulled any picture from the file marked "Black Militant Women." During the next segment the reporter apologized for the error. He said, "We showed a picture of Kathleen Cleaver during a story about Angela Davis. We didn't realize how much they look alike, but really they do." Don't they all?

Robert Singleton, an economics professor and ex-head of UCLA's Afro Studies program, paid great attention to the press reaction to Angela. He feels that people saw an aura developing around her. Whites saw a situation in which, potentially, all black militants would come together. A lot of people, he thinks, know that if all blacks joined to declare war on racism, a dangerous situation would develop. Angela could have been that center around which people would rally. This was recognized, and it frightened people—establishment press, liberals, all kinds. Too much change coming too fast. "The black change agent," Bob Singleton goes on, "he's recognized, and the moment he develops the kind of

* *The New York Times*, October 16, 1970.

charisma Malcolm had, the kind Angela was getting, they blow him away." Considering Angela's own reaction to the press, he adds, "She always stayed herself even though she was trying very hard to rise to the occasion that was growing around her. Ultimately what she really was was a girl aware of the monstrosity that newspapers were making her into. She was definitely afraid that the monstrosity would somehow prevail, that it would live beyond her."

PART II/THE SOUTH:
GROWING UP

1/BOMBINGHAM, ALABAMA

"We blindly accepted the proposition that Negroes were inferior and should therefore be kept in their place—the back of the bus, the balcony of the theater, the 'nigger bleachers' at the ball park and in their own churches and schools and restaurants. . . ."

—Paul Hemphill

Angela Yvonne Davis was born on January 26, 1944, in Birmingham, Alabama, a town local residents have nicknamed "Bombingham." For Angela and her family that city was more than just a town to live in: the facts of Birmingham influenced every aspect of life if you were black, and the facts were devastating. There was a Chamber of Commerce sign at the approach to the city which read, "It's so nice to have you in Birmingham." For Angela, and for Ben born in 1945, for their younger sister, Fania, and little brother, Reggie, who were born in 1947 and 1950, it wasn't so nice to be in Birmingham. It was a city that sounded like bombs exploding across the street late at night. It was their parents saying, "We're in a hurry," when they passed Kiddyland: the fun fair was any child's vision of heaven, but blacks were not allowed to enter. Downtown was a place where the drinking fountains were marked "white" and "colored" and where salesgirls were gleefully insolent to Mrs. Davis.

"People took every opportunity to be rude to us," Mrs. Sallye Davis remembers. Buying a foundation garment one day, she wrote a check and the shopgirl, looking at it, grinned and said, "Thank you, Sallye." Mrs. Davis explained firmly that she was not in the habit of having strangers address her by her first name. "Aren't you, Sallye?" replied the girl. Only when Mrs. Davis suggested that she would return the garment did the girl apologize hastily. It was one of a thousand incidents that went unnoticed by the prosperous white population of Birmingham. For them it was a growing city, a boomtown, a "good place to live in."

"The striking thing about Birmingham is that it seems so advanced industrially and so retarded politically," wrote James Reston of the *New York Times*. "Birmingham was, and is, the major center for iron and steel production in the South. But the impression is of a city which had been trapped for decades in a Rip Van Winkle slumber."

Birmingham seems very green as you first approach it, almost a countrified town, though the steel mills belch black clouds in the distance. Even early in April the trees are in full bloom, the leaves and grass so rich in color that the green appears tinged with opulent veins of blue. The earth, where bulldozers have left scars, is deep red, almost bloody in the spectacular sunset. Big shade trees line the streets, comforting the big handsome houses and the rows of unpainted shacks in the violent heat that comes early, pushing the June temperatures past ninety. The verdant foliage, the warm climate, the smalltown feeling are in sharp contrast to the busy efficiency of the production line. A statue of Vulcan, the symbol of Birmingham, dominates the town. From the Davis backyard you can see it with its red light at night to proclaim an accident that day, green to say all is well.

From its birth around the 1880s Birmingham has always been a young, growing, hustling kind of place, nourished by rich deposits of iron ore, coal, and bauxite. From the beginning its lifelines were the railroads. It grew into a major export center with the development of water trains that rushed products to the Gulf. By 1950, when Angela was six, the population had soared to over three hundred thousand. Skyscrapers went up in the pre-Depression boomtime 1920s. New houses covered the pleasant countryside, new schools full of shiny new equipment and furniture were built. Black schools got the hand-me-downs. Mrs. Davis recalls that when a new school for whites went up, the battered old furniture went to an old school for blacks. When she first started teaching in 1939–40, Mrs. Davis earned $53.60 a month. There were no materials at all for the children in black schools; anything they got came out of the teacher's salary.

The median income was high for the country then—$2500—but black families earned a great deal less. Statistics show that in 1949 nearly 39 percent of blacks in the South earned less than $500 a year and only 2.9 percent earned the median income for Birmingham whites.

Although the Davis family was by no means at the bottom of the financial heap, there were times when they discussed moving from the South. The facts of segregated life were far from pleasant, and segregation was total when Angela and Ben and Fania were growing up. Mrs. Davis said to her husband then, "If it was just the two of us, we could stick it out, but we ought to think of the children." Mr. B. Frank Davis wasn't easily convinced: "We'll think about that later," he would say. What he really meant, in his gentle, understated way, was that nobody, white or black, was going to make him move out of his house, away from his town, no matter how tough things got. And at times they got very tough indeed.

The Davis children grew up under Eugene ("Bull") Connor's reign of terror. Bull Connor, Commissioner of Public Safety from 1936 to 1963, ran the segregation system so efficiently that few white people even recognized "the balance of the races" as an issue. Any threat of change galvanized the town into action, however, and suspicion that the order of things was being questioned provoked brutal reprisal. There were subtler methods of maintaining the status quo: the signs, the back of the bus, the separate but very unequal classrooms. A legal code existed, talmudic in its all-inclusive instructions on how to conduct a segregated way of life. It was, for example, a violation for a black person to sleep in a white person's house. When twelve-year-old Angela tried to organize an interracial talk group at her Sunday school, police broke it up. Fania has memories of trying to sit at the front of the bus, beyond the board separating the races, while her mother beckoned her to the back. Fania would simply jump into the first seat. Mrs. Davis, unable to bring herself to tell her own children they mustn't, couldn't, shouldn't do this or that because of their skin color, would say, "Come back here." "Why, because it's too hot up here?" Fania would demand. "Yes," Mrs. Davis answered, "because it's too hot."

Connor acquired such power in his twenty-seven-year rule that his police department was virtually an autonomous state within a state. Of course, it was often pointed out, black people did pretty well for themselves in Birmingham. There were more educated blacks than in many Southern cities, more of them had jobs, there was a sizable middle class. But it was a bit like showing the world a shiny new bus and saying, "See, black folks can ride in there," without adding that those same black folks could ride only in the back, and that there wasn't anywhere much they could go once they got off.

To white people, blacks inhabited a second-class world apart. It wasn't articulated, Angela remembers, but the white person was the enemy. There was plenty of envy for what they had, the hostility to the whites was intense, but there was no direct contact at all. As late as 1967, when

Reggie, the only Davis to attend an integrated school, went to Ensley High, life was very hard for him. The school was nominally integrated, but the cafeteria, the classrooms, the students, were automatically separated into white and black. Racism was still a highly institutionalized way of life.

With each hint of protest from the black community—starting with its infiltration into white neighborhoods in the late 1940s—Connor intensified his program of terror. Police brutality went unchallenged. Once federal laws on integration were passed, city officials did indeed recognize them: rather than permit the Metropolitan Opera to play to integrated audiences, they canceled its annual tour; rather than allow blacks to use them, they closed the parks to everyone. With the beginnings of real resistance in the 1950s and early 1960s it was said that church bombings adequately immunized the black population from the civil rights contagion. For "white people had to make a decision: fight desegregation or work for it," Paul Hemphill, a writer born in Birmingham says. ". . . the sight of those uppity folks actually demanding service in white Southern restaurants during the early sixties drove him (my old man) into a frenzy. This wasn't my old man. It was somebody else. An autographed eight-by-ten of George Wallace showed up on the family piano. He talked about reactivating his father's old squirrel rifle which hadn't been fired in at least forty years. Funny things were happening in the Family. After being bombarded by Freedom Riders and Martin Luther King, church bombers and police dogs, it seemed as if everybody in Birmingham—you must visit sometime, really 'It's Nice to have you in Birmingham'—was preparing to give the world twenty-four hours to get out of town."

Bombs were a well-tested and officially sanctioned white racist weapon. By the 1960s, when more than sixty or seventy bombings had occurred, when officials admitted that they "knew" who had perpetrated them, not a single person had been brought to trial. There were the police dogs too, and the firehoses. For the Davis family bombs going off had become a way of life.

In 1948 the Davises moved into an area zoned for whites, thus breaking local ordinances that divided Birmingham's residential areas along racial lines. They were part of a general trend: houseowning whites were anxious to sell, newly prosperous black families were eager to buy; and in the bargaining the regulations were—deliberately or otherwise—overlooked. Once the deeds were signed, however, blacks were accused of violating the zoning laws. A prominent City Council member promised, "There's going to be bloodshed," in a tone that was an invitation to violent reprisals against blacks. The sound of bombs going off is written clearly in the memories of all the Davis children—as are the "colored" signs on buses and in bathrooms and coffee shops. There was no escape.

Dynamite Hill, they called the neighborhood where the Davis family came to live. It was an attractive place—almost countryside, with only a few houses set among trees and open fields where the children could play. There was a drawback, however. Every evening men drove slowly along Center Street, throwing explosives at the houses. Mr. Davis and his neighbors began to patrol the area. They stationed a truck down the hill near their church, another in a lot across from the Davis home. If someone suspicious drove up the hill, the men near the church radioed a warning. Mr. Davis recalls long hours when he and the others kept watch until dawn. The police came some of the time. Crowds would gather whenever there was a bombing. But the police rarely looked for the culprit, only used their guns to prod local black people back inside their houses. One evening, for no reason at all, an officer called Angela's brother Ben from the front porch and searched him. Another night a bomb went off in the house next door. Mrs. Davis felt the whole house shake—china rattled, furniture bounced—so hard that she thought her own house had been hit and that it was all over. She and her mother-in-law grabbed the children and ran out into the street. It was the middle of the night. The Davis house survived this and other incidents intact, a fact that Angela ascribed to luck. "We live on the right side of the street, don't we?" she noted. "We haven't been bombed yet."

The bombings came in waves. When black families first moved onto the hill, explosives were set in the hope of blowing them off. After the 1954 School Desegregation Act the fear of integration provoked whites to further violence. Birmingham was not a town where warnings were verbal: they came in the shape of bombs and they were deadly. During Martin Luther King's era of resistance, more and more explosions were heard in the night. A neighbor, Arthur Shores, who defended Autherine Lucy, the first black woman to attend the University of Alabama, was bombed out of his house three times. Mrs. Davis recalls how for years she checked carefully among the shrubs in her front yard: she was looking for the green boxes filled with explosives and hidden in the bushes near the homes of black people. The Green Box Bombings were followed by yet another wave of violence. Just before the Civil Rights Act of 1964 was signed, the prospect of black people in their restaurants and hotels so terrorized the white population that they flung yet more bombs; all too often the victims were, even by racist criteria, the most innocent.

On September 15, 1963, Mrs. Davis received a panic-stricken call from one of her neighbors. Would Mrs. Davis drive her down at once to the 16th Street Baptist Church? There had been a disaster of some kind, and she was afraid for her little girl, Cynthia, an only child, who was at Sunday school. As the two women drove up to the church Mrs. Davis saw that the stained-glass windows had been blown out into the street and that part of the building had been reduced to rubble. A crowd had gathered. Women were screaming and crying and searching among the rubble for their missing children.

That morning a bomb had been planted in the basement of the church, Birmingham's biggest black church and a focus for civil rights activities. In the middle of the Sunday school session the bomb went off. Cynthia Wesley and three other little girls—all from the neighborhood, all friends of the Davis children—were found eventually, their bodies shattered by the explosion; no one knew how quickly they had died that morning.

Against the background of terror the Davises stood firm. What made them special was that they kept their self-respect in a world that degraded you because of your color. Instead of choosing to go elsewhere and live a quiet life, as they could have done, they stayed in the South at a time when— hard as it is to imagine today, less than twenty years later— dogs attacked children in the streets who were attempting to drink a cup of coffee at Walgreen's. A friend, David Poindexter, comments, "That took a special quality. The whole family has it, that special innate sense of dignity. It was programed into all the kids, and they carry it with grace. When Mr. Davis bought his house on the top of the hill and people were throwing dynamite, he knew that it was his house. It was the house where his family lived and where he meant his kids to grow up and have as good a life as he could give them. No one was going to make him run. He intended to take care of his family and his commitment to the community. He wasn't afraid."

"The missionary teachers from New England, fresh from the then recent victories of Horace Mann and Henry Barnard in the battle for a free public school, encouraged the freedom in their conviction. At no time or place in America has there been exemplified so pathetic a faith in education as the level of racial progress. Grown men studied their alphabets in the fields holding the blue back speller with one hand while they guided the plow with the other. Mothers tramped scores of miles to towns where they could place their children in school. Pine torches illumined the dirt floored cabins where men, women and children studied until far into the night. No mass movement has been more in the American tradition than the urge which drove Negroes toward education seen after the Civil War."

—E. Franklin Frazier *quoting* Horace Mann Bond

"They are the All-American family on a newer and better model. They lived and raised their children according to the American dreams, the middle-class way of life. Yet they never ignored the world around them. They never let their principles go to get a piece of the goods. It was vitally important in the way Angela learned to think and feel," Haywood Burns said of the Davises.

Angela Yvonne, Fania Elizabeth, Benjamin Frank, Jr., and Reginald Wayne Davis grew up in the large, comfortable white frame house on the hill at the corner of North 11th Court and Center Street. It is a lived-in house, one that has settled peacefully with age into the neighborhood. From the upstairs windows you can look out over Birmingham and to the lush green hills in the distance. Trees in the yard shade the clapboard house and the deep porch that runs the whole way around it. The houses next door and across the

25

street are newer, large modern red-brick structures that have replaced with that of peaceful suburbia the countrylike atmosphere that the Davises first knew in 1948. Not far away, down the hill, is the service station Mr. Davis owns and where he works long hours; coming back up the road, you pass crude housing for the very poor and ramshackle huts with tarpaper roofs for the even poorer. You can't see them from the top of the hill. In the other direction is the First Congregationalist United Church of Christ—Mrs. Davis' church; Tuggle Elementary School, which all the Davis children attended, is only a few blocks away. It is a close-knit neighborhood: everyone seems to know everyone else in this part of town. Mrs. Davis waves constantly to familiar faces as cars pass, and there is always a Coke or a glass of milk or a cup of coffee for the friends who often drop by. Neighborhood children are magnetically drawn to Mrs. Davis and she welcomes them all, not only with love but with pleasure in their company.

Everyone comes in at the back door: the kitchen is the nerve center of the house, it is Mrs. Davis' territory. It is a big friendly yellow room crowded with appliances, the smells of something good cooking, the sounds of talk and laughter and children. Beyond it is the dining room. An old demitasse set sits on a sideboard—the room seems ready for the next family gathering. The walls are hung with diplomas—school and college degrees, mentions of honors fill every space. You pass on into a big comfortable sitting room that shows the marks of a big family and long years of use. There are college yearbooks on the coffee table, and in the front hall athletic trophies vie for attention with portraits of the Davis children. A photo of Angela as a pretty college sophomore smiles out at you. In the study are shelves of books left behind as each of the Davises departed for school and then college. The walls are covered with "Free Angela" posters, drawings, and sketches sent by a dozen different young artists, photographs of her, letters and postcards from France and Germany and Russia. Mrs. Davis collects them now as proudly as she has gathered testaments to all the achievements of her children.

Upstairs Angela's bedroom window gives onto a panorama of the quiet countryside. As the eldest in the family she marked the path the others would follow. She was, Mrs. Davis says, grinning at her own nervousness as a young mother, a "book baby." Mrs. Davis was careful to put her in a playpen and she rarely crawled, but she walked at an early age, much like her niece, Angela Aisa (Fania's daughter), who is staying now with Mr. and Mrs. Davis. Laughing, Mrs. Davis said she was considerably less anxious when the others came along. As the oldest, Angela was also the leader. When Ben learned that his sister, at fifteen, was leaving home for high school, he said with a smile, "Now I'm going to be king!"

Mrs. Sallye Davis is a small, very pretty woman who was clearly a great force in the lives of her four children growing up in Birmingham. She carries herself with great and natural dignity, her eyes are filled with kindness but they are sharply intelligent too and miss little. There is an air of great strength and determination about her that is tempered by a broad sense of humor. Her face often relaxes into a wide smile and often the smile grows and explodes into laughter. Both of her daughters look like her, although as a small child Angela took after her father. Mrs. Davis calls Birmingham home, though she comes from Caladiga County about fifty miles away. As a high-school student she was forced to move to Birmingham—there was no school in her county. Her college days were spent here too, and later she spent summers in New York gaining a master's degree at New York University. Smiling, she admits she met her husband in a Birmingham public library.

The family doesn't talk about it, but the fact that B.

Frank Davis was the son of a black mother and a white father has had a profound effect on them. In the much-quoted letter to George Jackson in prison Angela showed her hatred of this white grandfather and the system he represented: "Rather than helplessly watch her children die a slow death of starvation, my grandmother submitted to the white master, my father's accursed father. . . ."

Born in Ringo County, a hundred miles from Birmingham, Mr. Davis taught school, like his wife, for many years before he took over the service station he now owns. He speaks in a very quiet voice. Talking of the bombings and the long nights watching, he shows little emotion. He keeps things to himself. He is matter-of-fact about the ways things were; he just did what had to be done. He is a kindly man, with courteous, almost old-fashioned manners, and both his quiet, gentle sons take after him. Temperamentally different from each other, Mr. and Mrs. Davis were, however, very much alike in their intense determination to educate their children and to do it well.

Mrs. Davis taught in a primary school when the children were small. Anxious to see them safe while she was away, she sent them to preschool programs, Angela and Ben when they reached the age of two and Fania at a little over one. She disliked not spending all her time with her children and felt dissatisfied if an evening passed when she could not read to them. All of the children learned to read very early, and Mrs. Davis played the word games with them that she played with her pupils at school. From a very early age Angela developed a tremendous curiosity about words, and whenever she saw a billboard or a magazine title, she would pester her parents to tell her, "What does that spell?" Angela was her daddy's little girl. "As the oldest," Mrs. Davis said, "she really knew how to handle her daddy. When they put her in jail, it hurt him terribly to see her subjected to such false charges."

The children went on to Tuggle Elementary School just down the road from the Davises', and then to Parker High, except for Reggie, who went to the integrated Ensley High School.

Angela did very well at school; but shy, she rarely raised her hand although she knew the answers. Her mother chided her, "How is anyone going to know if you know the answer if you don't tell them?" Fania, much more outspoken than her older sister, would say just what she had on her mind. Angela, Mrs. Davis says, was the soul of tact, but Fania often had to be reminded that tact was a useful possession. An avid reader, Angela rarely went anywhere without a book. If Mrs. Davis took her visiting and the adult chatter went on a little too long, she'd pull a book from her bag, settle back, and begin to read. Her concentration was at times too intense; often she withdrew to her own room to finish a project, only to be reminded by her mother that it would also be nice to see some friends or go to a party. What she began she finished, and Angela could forget entirely what was happening around her and simply go on with her intellectual work. Of her shyness Angela says, "I tended to be on the quiet side. I still am, I think. But it is not easy for me to paint an objective picture of those things. It depended on the situation and what I felt was required of me, how I related to other people. You could probably find others who would tell you that I was the most aggressive, outgoing kind of person. A lot of people I knew even accused me of being too 'domineering,' of trying to control things."

According to their mother, the children were alike in many ways, but eventually each took a different path. Ben and Reggie, for example, believed in freedom and justice as much as anyone else, but they took a quieter route, perhaps because they had not traveled as much around the world as their sisters. Final decisions were left to the children in the

Davis family, although Mrs. Davis strongly suggested what she thought right. And in some things she was very firm: she set high standards and she expected her children to live up to them. One of these was the practice of religion.

The First Congregationalist United Church of Christ was just down the hill, and it was there the family went every Sunday, although Mr. Davis was an Episcopalian and Angela had been christened in his church. All three older children were confirmed together, even Fania, who was only eight but was determined not to be left out on the big day; she had fulfilled all the requirements, so the Reverend Long, the young minister, gave in to Fania's persuasion. When young, the children were dedicated churchgoers, but as they got older they got lazier about Sunday morning church school. Mrs. Davis would carefully hint that unless everyone got ready, that if there was no church school that day, there just might not be any outings either. To this day, when the family is home together, Mrs. Davis likes to see them all at church together.

Reverend Long was a very young man and very modern, intensely involved with civil rights and always working to make the church relevant. As well as square dancing for the younger members of the church, there were groups in which they discussed subjects such as the right Christian approach to the oppression they were suffering.

The children pursued a whole range of other activities, occasionally prodded by their mother. A friend who knew Angela later remarked, "She wouldn't have been half as compulsive without the pushing and prodding by her mother." Scouting was one activity. All four Davis children were Scouts—the girls Brownies and later Girl Scouts, the boys Cubs and Boy Scouts. The local Girl Scout unit was very good and Angela was a very good member of it, winning a great many badges. She was one of eight Alabama girls—four black, four white—chosen to go to the National Girl Scout Round-up in Colorado, an honor Fania was to receive in her turn. Angela came away from scouting with a certain passion for leathercraft. Mrs. Davis and a neighbor finally broke down and bought tooling sets for their daughters, and an almost endless stream of wallets, moccasins, and belts began to appear in the neighborhood, only to dry up when Angela, like any American girl, grew too sophisticated for the Scouts.

There were dancing lessons and music lessons. Angela was the most musical of all, and she "was doing really well" when she gave it up at fifteen, her mother lamented. She studied the clarinet but changed to the saxophone in high school to fill a vacancy in the school band. At one stage Angela tried to teach Ben to dance. "She didn't," Ben says with a grin, "have much luck."

There were family trips and vacations to New England, California, and Colorado, but in the minds of the four Davis children the best time of all was summer in New York.

Still attending New York University to work for her master's degree, Mrs. Davis each summer took the children with her so that they could make use of what the city offered and visit their aunts there.

There wasn't any place for a black child to swim in the scorching Alabama summers. New York, with its YMCA pools, its beaches, and lakes not far upstate, was paradise. NYU ran a school for the children of its summer students and there the young Davises learned all kinds of things— sewing, music, dancing, gymnastics. Their aunts took them to the Statue of Liberty and to Orchard Beach, to the United Nations when they were older, and to the Bronx Zoo, where you could ride on llamas and camels. The city was exciting, it was alive, and it was full of things to do. There wasn't, in fact, anything a kid couldn't do in New York because she was black. There were all kinds of things to see and do, to eat and smell, there was freedom. Coming back to Birmingham when summer ended and seeing the out-of-bounds local Howard Johnson's, Ben would sigh and say, "All I want to do is get back to New York to get to Howard Johnson's." When summer came again, he forgot about Howard Johnson's—it was the lure of the forbidden that made him long for New York. Then he came up with a solution: Ben said to his mother, "Why can't we just stay in New York?" "What about Daddy?" she replied. "Well, he can come too," Ben said, having worked it all out. "But what about the house?" "Well, why can't we just move the house up there too?" As a fifth-grader Angela had a poem to write. Though she rarely came to her parents for help, she found herself stuck and asked advice. "Think about last summer," her mother said. "Oh, yes," Angela said, her face lighting up. Fania sighed, "I wish I were a bird; then I'd fly back to New York."

It was always very difficult and at times more than she could bear for Mrs. Davis to explain just why Ben could go into Howard Johnson's in New York and not in Birmingham. The Davises did not try to shield their children from the facts once they were old enough to comprehend them, but when they were small, their mother feared that the harsh truths of Southern life might make them insecure. "How can you tell your six-year-old he can't drink water from a fountain because of the color of his skin?" she says. Life proceeded in an orderly way; Mrs. Davis protected her children as best she could, but she could not isolate them from the sounds of bombs or the sight of signs that said "Colored." Her greatest fear was that her children would grow to hate others. She explained that there was good in people of all races, that you must not hate anyone. It is, to her, a much better idea to pray for them. Mrs. Davis is a woman who believes that you cannot sleep if there is hatred in your heart.

"Angela was brought up to be a lady, to be a nice Negro girl who would fit comfortably into the black bourgeoisie," wrote Ingrid Bengis, Angela's classmate at Brandeis. Which is true—but only to a limited extent, and especially to an outsider. All too often Angela has been identified as a nice little bourgeois girl who went bad. Angela and her family do not fall neatly into categories: they are hard to label. Though they lived a middle-class life and cultivated middle-class tastes for books and music, there was little pretension: they did what interested them. Status was not only unimportant but irrelevant, and they did not hesitate to risk their way of life by taking up the cause of less well-established blacks. When the children pointed out their neighbors' brand-new shiny houses and complained about the old-fashioned dowdiness of their own, Mrs. Davis retorted sharply that they were not interested in keeping up with the Joneses. Education came in a very strong first, well ahead of swimming pools. In contrast there was, Mrs. Davis remarks, a desperate desire for status and its symbols among many middle-class black families she knew—just like everyone else in America, and more.

E. Franklin Frazier wrote in his penetrating study, *The Black Bourgeoisie*:

> The entire history of the Negro in the United States has been of a nature to create in the Negro a feeling of racial inferiority. Two centuries of slavery, the legalized system of segregation shortly after the Civil War, have established this. . . . The Black Bourgeoisie is the element which has striven more than any

other among Negroes to make itself over in the image of the white man, and exhibits most strikingly the inferiority complex of those who would escape their racial identification.

There was what Angela calls "the whole gamut of imitations of white social life. Piano lessons, ballet lessons, until you reach the caricatured debutante affairs. I don't want to sound so cynical—because if you think about it, it is not very difficult to pinpoint the precise forces which led to such developments. And these forces, too, are definitely part of our oppression as Black people; at the same time what I have called imitations of white social life were a feeble effort to move toward something like Black nationhood."

Mrs. Davis remembers that she too, proud of her bright and charming daughters, had hopes of presenting them to society. It would be done through her social club and not expensively. But the decision was left to the girls. Mrs. Davis talked it over with Angela, who reacted strongly against the whole idea. "Oh, no, Mother, it's too much money," and that was that. When a friend had a huge coming-out party with all the frills, Angela and Fania found it a terrible waste. They would much rather travel. Frazier describes the balls:

> The fantastic accounts of the achievements of Negroes and recognition accorded them by whites constitute important elements in the world of make believe which the Negro press has created to compensate for the feelings of inferiority of the Black Bourgeoisie. It is a society that has status without substance. . . . In cities all over the country, Negro society has inaugurated Debutante Balls or Cotillions which provide an opportunity every year for the so-called rich Negroes to

indulge in lavish expenditure and create a world of fantasy to satisfy their longing for recognition. Despite the tinsel, glitter and gaiety of the world of make believe in which middle class Negroes take refuge, they are still beset by feelings of insecurity and frustration. As a consequence the free and easy life which they appear to lead is a mask for their unhappy existence.

"A man," Booker T. Washington said, "never begins to have self-respect until he owns his own home." The black bourgeoisie into which Angela was born had the trappings of middle-class America, but not the economic basis that would give those trappings roots in the world of reality. In the period up to 1960; 80 percent of the so-called black bourgeoisie owned beauty parlors, barbershops, undertaking establishments, and other service businesses. In 1951 there were fourteen banks owned by blacks, the biggest employing fifteen people.

Piety, thrift, and respectability were the legacy left to the South by the teachers and missionaries of New England. One ambition was to live chastely, thus disproving white charges of animal instincts; another was to speak English correctly, thereby distinguishing yourself from the masses. People must be able to recognize "There goes a college boy or girl." When industrialization brought new chances of wealth, the black bourgeoisie kept the trappings of these values, but money became the real measure of achievement. And with every dollar white America mustered for organizations like the United Negro College Fund, it promoted this attitude. Of the post-Second World War generations of the black bourgeoisie, Frazier writes, "They have been taught that money will bring them justice and equality in American life, and they propose to get money."

Gertrude Stein declared that American blacks, having

lost the "very ancient but very narrow culture" of their African forebears, "were suffering from nothingness." In Frazier's view she would have been nearer the truth if she had applied this "nothingness" to the black bourgeoisie in particular, rather than to American blacks in general. "When Negroes attain middle-class status," he wrote, "their lives generally lose both content and significance."

As she grew into adolescence Angela began, however inarticulately, to react impatiently to the trappings and pretenses of the middle-class blacks she knew and indignantly to the violent injustices of a racist society. When at fifteen she had the opportunity to leave home for New York, she took the chance. Mrs. Davis was uncertain. Angela had already been admitted to nearby Fisk University in Nashville, where her mother "could hop in the car any weekend" to see her. And, by starting college at an early age, she would have a head start in the long medical school course she planned to take. Mr. Davis and Reverend Long urged Mrs. Davis to let her go north. Let her take the bigger opportunity for a better background, Mr. Davis said. Scared of the big city, of the drugs and the freedom, Mrs. Davis was reassured when she met the Melish family who were designated by the American Friends Southern Negro Student Committee to play host to her daughter in New York. There were doubts even then, for Angela had never done any single dating. There were always lots of friends at home, Mrs. Davis recalls; Angela could have anyone at all around to the house. "One little guy," she remembered, "asked me if he could take her to a prom." Mrs. Davis said she would drive them both there and, as she was to be a chaperone at the dance, bring them both home again.

Togetherness was an important, the essential, fact of life in the Davis family. Angela explains that her mother felt almost that "some sacred taboos would be violated" if the family didn't vacation together and, later on, when the children left home, if they didn't reassemble every Christmas. The hardest Christmas of all, Mrs. Davis said quietly, was the second one Angela spent in jail. Everyone suggested they dispense with the ritual of turkey and dressing: the empty place at the table was too visible. Then Reggie announced that some turkey would certainly taste good and Mrs. Davis began to prepare the traditional feast. When the telephone rang, it was Angela, who had been permitted to call, and later, Mrs. Davis confesses, after she had heard her child's voice, her appetite slowly returned.

As she grew up and grew away from the tightly knit family circle, Angela began to look for another kind of solidarity to replace it. For though "there was something very strange about vacations" when she came home from New York with sophisticated notions shocking to her friends and family, and though, having read and discussed all kinds of new ideas at school, she felt estranged from the life her parents were living, she still somehow wanted to stay at home. There was a deep yearning to belong to her own people. Her feelings were still nebulous and unarticulated, but "in general I think I always harbored a real desire to stay there; there is a different quality of relations between black people. Something that must be the result of centuries of fighting off oppression."

3/OUT OF A TRADITION

"Watch the socialists. We may not follow them and agree with them in all things—I certainly do not. But in trend and ideal they are the salt of this present earth. In the socialist trend lies the one great hope of the Negro American."

—W.E.B. DuBois

Angela did not simply spring up a fully formed radical from a politically arid middle-class wasteland. Nor did she "go through half my life oblivious to what was going on around me and then suddenly see the light." Her intellectual precocity and tastes, the poverty and discrimination that she witnessed (and experienced), her distaste for the escape route to "okay status," her contacts with Communists when she was young gave her an early predisposition toward some form of socialism. From her parents she inherited a perceptive social conscience: their involvement with the first stirrings of the civil rights movement provided a basic model. And they were part of a long, strong tradition of what Haywood Burns called "Help the Race," a "radical" tradition of black activism in the South as old as the slave rebellions. Within this tradition the Marxists played a small but definitive part.

The tradition of black radicalism in the South goes back to Nat Turner and Gabrielle Prosser. There were such famous political figures as Frederick Douglass; there were those who worked in the Populist cause in the late nineteenth century. Boycotts began, not with Martin Luther King, but in the early years of this century when blacks refused to ride on streetcars. The National Association for the Advancement of Colored People (NAACP) was considered radical, even extremist, when it was organized in the first years of the 1900s. The twentieth century brought organizations such as the Southern Negro Youth Congress to which both Mr. and Mrs. Davis belonged as college students. Later there was King's Southern Christian Leadership Conference (SCLC) and there was the Congress of Racial Equality (CORE). In retrospect this does not seem like a radical tradition, but "radical" is a relative term. In the 1930s and 1940s one might be subjected to harassment simply for speaking out against the racist order of things. To the established white supremacists, these black people were a far greater threat than today's student Maoist is to Richard Nixon. Black Communism in the South was less clear and less defined simply because black Marxists were not very visible. "It would have been suicide for them to be so," Haywood Burns said. But the Communist Party did play a role, and not all of its members were invisible.

Clearly the Communists saw black people, the most oppressed group in America, as likely recruits. Black people, on the other hand, quickly recognized how the Communist Party could be useful to them, and from there it was often only a short step to joining up. In fact, the Left Wing in general tended to romanticize them, seeing them, in the words of Harold Cruse, author of *The Crisis of the Negro Intellectual*, as "a beautiful untarnished and noble folk struggling for equality." With this vision in mind, the Party set itself in the 1920s and 1930s to take the blacks over, and in the attempt, as Frazier pointed out, it provided them with part of their political education: "The Communists began to attack the religiosity and other-worldly outlook of the Negro masses. They organized Negroes in demonstrations against racial discrimination; they nominated Negroes for political office; they gave special attention to Negro workers in their attempt to capture organized labor." And in this drive for black recruitment the party had some success. Four planks made the party's platform one on which politically aggressive blacks felt they could reasonably stand up as men. An attack on all forms of racial oppression; denunciation of the black intellectuals and bourgeoisie for allegedly supporting the interests of white capitalists against the interests of the race; a call for united revolutionary action on the part of both white and black workers against the capitalist class; self-determination for the Black Belt—a proposal to carve out an all-Negro forty-ninth state from the heart of the South.

But as the Communists made gains among the blacks they also provoked a two-pronged attack against themselves: from the authorities and from black-middle-class leaders, especially preachers. The Communists had attacked the blacks' Christian resignation and the Christian preachers fought back. "Because of their traditional religious background," Frazier writes, "the Negro masses were easily persuaded by Negro preachers that the irreligious Communists were using Negroes as tools." Black Communist activists were subjected by the lay authorities to extraordinary brutality. To be persecuted it was enough simply to be a Party member. The idea that if one black went "red," the rest might follow terrified the whites, suggested Frank M. Davis, the black editor of the *Atlanta World*: "Twelve million backed by the USSR would be too big a group to deal with by force." So force had to be used first; subversion had to be nipped in the bud; the Communists had to be outlawed and any little sign of uppity protest had to be neutralized and negated under the general label of Communism. Mrs. Davis remembers that when anyone spoke out on an issue, no matter how mildly, he was labeled a Communist. So violent were the reactions to the Communists that many blacks remained silent on all issues for sheer fear of being called Communist.

But if the Communists never made great inroads on the blacks, they did, however, represent a channel for political activism long before the civil rights movement began. They provided a well-defined platform and, more importantly, they rushed to the support of those persecuted for their color.

The Communist Party proved itself publicly as the defender of black people in several notable instances in which injustice had been done, attracting, with its strong organization and worldwide connections, the indignation of thousands. One such instance provides a striking parallel to the case of Angela Davis, even down to the name of the central character: the case of Angelo Herndon.

Angelo Herndon, a black Birmingham coal miner who joined the Communist Party in the 1930s, became a *cause célèbre*. Because of his political affiliation, he was charged with "inciting to insurrection" and sentenced to twenty years on a chain gang. Its civil-liberties aspects prompted wide support for the case and it was an effective focus around which the Communists in the mid-1930s created a united front.

In "You Can't Kill the Working Class," a pamphlet he wrote to explain the appeal of the Communist Party to the black worker, Herndon talked of his life. Eugene Angelo Braxton Herndon was born to be a miner. His father was a miner, the sons never doubted they too would go down the mines. "The wail of the mine whistle morning and night and the sight of my father coming home with his lunch pail, grimy from the day's coating of coal dust, seemed a natural and eternal part of your lives." Herndon's parents had come from Birmingham to settle in Ohio at a time when every working-class family nursed the idea that one of its members would get out of the factory or the mine, sit at a desk, wear clean clothes. All the sacrifices were made for Angelo as a boy, but his father died of miner's pneumonia, leaving his mother with six other boys, two girls, and not much work except rich folks' housework. By the time Herndon was thirteen, he knew he would never make it to college, and he and his brother Leo went to Lexington, Kentucky, where there were mines, "and we were miners' kids."

Life in the company town meant low pay, nothing good to eat, nowhere good to sleep. It was there that the Jim Crow system first hit Herndon: blacks and whites lived in separate quarters, they worked in different parts of the mine. Blacks got the worst jobs, the first pay cuts, the role of scapegoat.

So Angelo and Leo set off for Birmingham, their father's hometown, where there was plenty of coal and still some relatives. They worked for the Tennessee Coal and Iron Railroad Co., which just about owned Alabama. Jim Crowism, stool pigeons—the TCI had them all. The TCI was like some "great greedy brute that held a whip over the whole state."

Herndon first learned about solidarity when, after one of the men was killed because of defective conditions, a whole group of miners quit for the day. Herndon spoke out when the company suggested the men whitewash the accident that was no accident. The truth was told; the dead man's family got some compensation.

He learned about the Communist Party through the blacks' word-of-mouth news system. "It was over this grapevine that we first heard that there were 'reds' in town. Bigtime Negroes and foremen said 'reds' were foreigners and Yankees and believed in killing people and would get us in trouble. I got a clear idea about the reds. They believed in organizing and sticking together. It all sounded OK."

"Would you rather fight or starve?" said the handbills Herndon saw in 1930. "It's war! It's war and I might as well get into it right now," Herndon throught to himself as he listened to a white man saying Negro and white workers had to stick together. He was followed by a Negro speaker—

from the same platform. From that day on Herndon's life became tied up with the workers' union. He joined the Unemployment Council and then the Communist Party; he read what literature he could find. "We Negroes want social equality and every other kind of equality. There's no reason on God's green earth why we should be satisfied with anything less."

Herndon "had always detested kowtowing" and being called "nigger." All of a sudden he had discovered an organization where Negroes and whites sat together. The leaders "were like us, the workers talked our language." Herndon was elected a delegate to the National Unemployment Convention in Chicago, whereupon his family kicked him out of the house. "My family had told me not to come back. What did I care? My real family was the organization. I'd found that I had brothers and sisters in every corner of the world. I knew that we were all fighting for one thing and that they'd stick by me. I never lost that feeling, in all the hard days to come, in Fulton Tower Prison with the threat of the electric chair and the chain gang looming over me."

One night in 1932 Herndon was grabbed, put in a cell, shown an electric chair and held incommunicado. His crime had been to call for mass demonstrations. The charge, inciting to insurrection, was rigged: it was based on a disused 1869 statute passed when Negroes were slaves. The law had lain unused. But now slaves of a new order were organizing, a crime punishable by death in the eyes of the "Georgia masters." At the trial on January 16, 1933, the state displayed literature taken from Herndon's room, read passages from it, and asked Herndon if he believed in Communist ideals. Yes, he replied, openly asserting his convictions. The state held that his membership in the Party and his possession of Communist literature were enough to send him to the electric chair.

And the hand-picked lily-white jury responded: "We,

the jury, find Angelo Herndon guilty." They sentenced him, not to death, but to eighteen to twenty years in jail. While the long months turned into long years, the Party mounted a campaign outside to draw attention to the injustice and in the end the campaign succeeded. Angelo Herndon had never lost faith. When he was arrested he wrote:

> They can hold this Angelo Herndon and hundreds of others but it will never stop these demonstrations on the part of Negro and white workers who demand a decent place to live in and proper food for their kids to eat. You may do what you will with Angelo Herndon. You may indict him. You may put him in jail. But there will come thousands of Angelo Herndons. If you really want to do anything about the case you must go out and indict the social system. But this you will not do, for your role is to defend the system under which the toiling masses are robbed and oppressed. You may succeed in killing one, two, even a score of working-class organizers. But you cannot kill the working class.

In the more notorious case of the Scottsboro Boys, the Communists came to the defense of nine black youths arrested in Jackson County, Alabama, in 1931. Although innocent—and in the end acknowledged to be so—they were charged with rape of two white girls, convicted and sentenced to the electric chair. They owed their freedom to the worldwide campaign of protest mobilized largely by the Communist Party. Forty years later, in 1970, the Party was again to organize international support, this time for Angela Davis.

In the 1940s, the Communist Party mounted a big campaign to save a black prison inmate from the gas chamber. The man, Warren Wesley Wells, faced execution for throwing a spittoon at a guard. The California penal code demanded the death sentence for any prisoner convicted of assaulting "a free man." The attorney who helped save Wells' life was a brilliant black man from Los Angeles named Lee Branton. In 1972, he defended Angela Davis and won her acquittal.

The "radical tradition" was the backdrop to Angela's political development. Factors in this development were the legacy of childhood in Birmingham, and the social, political, and particularly the familial actuality in which she lived. She began to identify with some of her parents' principles, and her family was impressively good; a family that gave its children great strength, integrity, and warmth. Mr. and Mrs. Davis had been involved in various activities well before Angela was born.

As college-student members of the Southern Negro Youth Congress, Mr. and Mrs. Davis attended conferences, conducted dialogue sessions to inform themselves on public issues and eventually to right unjust acts. Admittedly there was more talk than action, but under Bull Connor's reign of terror action was scarcely possible. Mrs. Davis, not a Communist herself, remembers going from door to door, gathering names for petitions in defense of the Scottsboro Boys. Among their friends in Birmingham were activists more militant than themselves, such as Louis Burnham (whose daughter Margaret was a childhood friend of Angela's and many years later one of her lawyers). Other local leaders whom the Davises knew were James Jackson and C. Herbert Oliver who documented police brutality. They were voices crying out in the wilderness. All were subjected to outrageous police harassment.

In the ranks of the black leaders—those who went North and those who stayed in Birmingham—were a few covert Party members. For very cogent reasons they didn't openly proclaim their allegiance, but the color of their political beliefs was no secret to their friends. Angela and her sister and brothers grew up with their children, and when still very young themselves learned this secret and began to understand something of its importance. From Angela's first childhood contact with it the Communist Party meant people her parents liked and respected. But Mr. and Mrs. Davis were never tempted to join the Party: the focus of their desire for change was more Christian than Communist.

In the late 1950s Mrs. Davis began to participate in boycotts and demonstrations; she worked with Martin Luther King's Southern Christian Leadership Conference. At her own church Reverend Long was a strong voice in organizations. Mrs. Davis was involved; she took part in church civil rights activities and she marched to protest segregation at the local department store.

But the social concern that Mrs. Davis passed on to Angela came not so much from her membership in organizations as from her own experiences as a teacher. Angela clearly recalls her feelings about children poorer than she, the kids who never had money to buy lunch or who missed school because the cardboard wouldn't keep the pebbles out of their shoes any longer. She was so disturbed by it that she would sometimes pick up change lying around the house for friends "who couldn't even afford to buy a bag of potato chips for lunch. When you're young it is hard to grasp why some people have enough—even too much—and others have nothing at all."

Though Mrs. Davis tried to protect her children from the despair and ugliness she saw among the desperately poor, though she admits that the tendency in the South was for people to keep their sons and daughters from associating with children of lower social or economic groups—those who wore the wrong clothes or spoke the wrong way—her own concern filtered through. Then too, the area just down the hill from the Davis home is terribly poor, its residents always in dire need. Seeing this, Angela would say, "We're just a little luckier than other people." Angela saw the hungry children in school, and she noticed that though her mother usually took only outgrown clothes to school, she sometimes took newer ones as well. Many of the children Mrs. Davis taught got a bath only if she gave them one. Taking along her own children's clothes, she would bathe her six- and seven-year-olds and dress them in clean skirts and trousers and shirts. Mrs. Davis' sensitive tact was revealed in the way she dealt with the problem of hand-me-downs sent to poor but proud parents. When she sent a freshly washed and clothed child home, she sent a little note to the parents with him. In it she explained that she had brought some of her children's things and she would be pleased if the parents kept them. Carefully she let them know that her own sons and daughters often received things that friends' children had outgrown. No parent ever sent back a garment that Mrs. Davis had given his child.

Many of the children ate almost nothing. There was one particularly hostile little boy in Mrs. Davis' first-grade class. Finally she went to his home: his mother had been taken off welfare; there was no food at all for the child who instead smoked what cigarette butts he could find. And so, long before the Black Panthers came up with it, Mrs. Sallye Davis invented the free breakfast. She cooked up big pots of grits and opened cans of beef, and after a year the little boy who had started it all was behaving better and beginning to learn. "After all," Mrs. Davis says, "you can't expect a child to learn on an empty stomach."

There were funny moments too in the family history of protest. When Angela and Fania came home on vacation, they often went downtown, chose a restaurant, sat anywhere, and began speaking very audibly in accomplished French. Confusion ensued: everyone wondered who they were and no one knew what to do with them.

Times have changed, but there are still plenty of racist reminders, Mrs. Davis remarked. A porter at United Airlines got to know the Davis family in 1971, when Mrs. Davis was flying around the country speaking out for Angela's freedom. He noticed the "Free Angela" sticker proudly plastered to Mr. Davis' car and asked for one for his own windshield. A few weeks later the company required him to remove it.

At fifteen, when Angela was ready to leave Birmingham for high school in the North, few of her political ideas had crystallized, but the "radical tradition," both historically and in her own family, predisposed her toward social criticism and perhaps also gave her the uplifting feeling—and the confidence—of knowing herself part of something larger than an individual, an historical trend with its sights fixed on the future. Perhaps Angela's later dislike of publicity came from this, from her desire to belong, to work hard as one part of a larger movement. Perhaps she became a leader in spite of herself.

After she left Alabama her early social concern and her instinctive feeling for socialism, coupled with an assertion of her own black identity, were to lead to her political involvements, to formal membership in a body working for change, to militant action.

When Angela was three, Mrs. Davis took her to hear Langston Hughes read his poetry at nearby Miles College. She sat very still through most of the performance. Afterward, at the reception, Mrs. Davis said, "Mr. Hughes, this is my daughter Angela." "I very much enjoyed your poems, Mr. Hughes. I know a poem too," Angela piped up, beginning to dance, " 'Mary had a little lamb. . . .' "

Many years later, when she had just been freed on bail in early spring 1971, Angela wrote a poem for her parents acknowledging a special debt to them: "All those years," she wrote, "you were getting me ready for my freedom fight."

PART III/GOING NORTH

4/AT HOME IN BROOKLYN

"We won round after round in our trial battles up to the point
when it looked like we might win. And then the Prize came
and with it looking like we might win—from that point on the
green light turned to a red light."

—THE REVEREND WILLIAM HOWARD MELISH

New York held no fears for Angela when she arrived in
1959. The memories of happy summers in the city reinforced
her enthusiasm, but did little to quell the nervous anticipation she felt about a new family, a new school, and an almost totally white world. Her vision of white people was
laden with all the things growing up in Alabama meant.
What the future held was unclear. It was the first break
from her tight-knit family; loneliness threatened.

Angela got her chance for a New York education from
the American Friends Southern Negro Student Committee,
an organization that annually took a number of promising
black boys and girls from the South to give them the best
that the American school system could offer. The chosen
youngsters were to be streamlined for Northern colleges—at
a time when to be accepted at all at a good college, a black
had to be not merely bright but superlatively so.

Ben never got to be "king" as he'd hoped when Angela
went away, leaving him the eldest and biggest in the family.
He too had been chosen by the American Friends to complete his schooling in the North, in Fairlawn, New Jersey, a
quiet suburban town where he lived with a gentle Quaker
family. Academically, the transition was very hard: the difference in standards between the Fairlawn schools and those

in Birmingham is vast. As the only black in the school, Ben often longed for familiar faces; at least in the city, he remarked, you can see blacks and all kinds of people on the subway. But Ben and Angela felt comforted to know that the other was just across the river: leaving home was not a total break.

In the transition from Birmingham to New York, Angela carried with her the notion that "things are better in the North." It wasn't until she had experienced what the white Northern world could hold that she realized her vision was a kind of myth and she herself a victim of it. The Melish family, however, was the exception. They were kind, generous, and welcoming people; the impact on Angela of living with a vitally political family was tremendous—what she learned and saw and felt in the Melish home stayed with her for a long time.

The Rev. and Mrs. William Howard Melish and their three sons, Billy, Jeff, and John, lived then at the corner of St. Mark's and Kingston Streets, in a comfortable, old house marking the dividing line between Bedford-Stuyvesant and Crown Heights. The neighborhood was in a state of New York flux. Once filled with white-middle-class Dutch and English families, it had then been invaded by immigrant Jews who, with prosperity, moved up from Williamsburg. Now, as Angela arrived, Puerto Ricans and Italians and blacks were moving in, making the neighborhood a vibrant, sometimes tense ethnic mix. Angela's new family put her at ease. They liked her gentleness, her good humor, and her kindness, noting that she was never self-absorbed, but always open to another's unhappiness and suffering. Settling in, she began to learn her way around the house in Brooklyn and around the city, and as well as liking her new family from the first, she began to develop a great admiration for them.

William Howard Melish was the minister of Trinity Episcopal Church, which under his father, the Rev. John Melish, had been one of the most popular churches in the "better" part of Brooklyn. After finishing his studies, William Melish joined his father as an assistant minister.

Believing after World War Two that the future would be shaped by postwar relations between the US and the USSR, William Melish helped organize Russian war relief, supported the United Nations strongly, and declared that despite differences in political and economic systems the two nations must learn to coexist peacefully. With this aim the National Council of American-Soviet Friendship was born, and after some time William Melish took over as chairman. When the council was put on the subversive list in 1947, Melish's bishop asked him to resign his chairmanship; he not only refused, but further annoyed his critics by visiting Yugoslavia to investigate the state of religious freedom and the circumstances surrounding the conviction of Archbishop Aloysius Stepinac. Meanwhile, Dr. John Melish had dismissed the subversive list as "illegal and unconstitutional." The upshot was a complaint from Trinity Church to the bishop and a request that both Melishes, father and son, quit their posts at Trinity, it being felt that a Republican congregation was entitled to a Republican rector. This move prompted a counterpetition from the pro-Melish section of the congregation: "We, the undersigned members of Holy Trinity parish, are completely opposed to the action of the vestry in asking for the resignation of our rector, Dr. John Howard Melish. We have the utmost affection for Dr. Melish and approve the policy he has consistently followed for the forty-five years of his rectorship. We state that the vestry in this action in no way represents our sentiments."

After hearings conducted by the hierarchy behind closed doors, the judgment was handed down: it was rejected that Dr. John Melish was too old, but maintained that there were serious dissensions in the parish which ". . . have an exhilarating effect on the whole Communist movement"! The Rector was charged with associating with "atheists, Communists, agitators of world revolution, totalitarianism and almost everything which denies the Christian doctrine of man." The case was taken to the Supreme Court of Kings County. Judge Meyer Steinbrink declared Reverend Melish removed. The case was appealed; a defense committee was set up; and father and son carried on the battle.

William Melish was determined to make Trinity a vital part of his changing neighborhood: when the blue-collar workers and the Puerto Ricans moved in, the white middle class felt threatened and began moving out. Melish invited his new neighbors to join his congregation, and the white and well-to-do grew angry: Melish had "defected." This only added bitterness to the battles between pastor and people. Eventually, as a concession, William Melish gave up his official position in the National Council of American-Soviet Friendship, but refused to resign his membership. A few colleagues, a few liberals, a few Jews protested. But his work was ruined, the church saw its effectiveness dwindle and finally had to shut its doors. Reverend Melish lost his church altogether.

The Melishes were still fighting in the courts when Angela reached New York. Money was running out. Their lives were constantly threatened with hate letters, ugly phone calls, vicious rumors. Angela must have learned a lot that would stand her in very good stead.

A large, easygoing man with an air of old-fashioned courtesy, William Melish is a very gentle person. He speaks softly, searching for the precise words. He is not bitter, but occasionally his eyes reveal someone who has lost what meant most. Mrs. Melish is pleasant and kindly-looking, but it is clear that she has no illusions left. Her eyes are kind but sharp, and describing their trials, she is far more direct and bitter than her husband. When they talk of Angela, there is nothing but warmth and affection in the air.

It was an exciting time when Angela came to Brooklyn, for though pressures often threatened to explode the family into desperation and shatter its stubborn resistance, the atmosphere was charged with the beginnings of the civil rights movement. An era of fear and silence seemed to be ending. Everyone in the house ate, breathed, and drank politics—there was the excitement of solidarity in the family. At meals the movement was discussed, tactics considered, positions pondered. Reverend Melish often explained the legal complexities of his own case, and political involvement was the emotional core of the household. There were the bad times as well. Angela learned about the perversity of the establishment, learned that the price of success in a political battle could be devastatingly high. For when the family had just about run out of money, Reverend Melish received a French Peace Prize. The money it carried provided for the family for nearly two years, as well as giving Melish new status. And then the tide turned. To see him win international accolades frightened Melish's enemies. People saw that he might win his battle, might regain his position, his church, and his influence. They made sure he didn't.

When William Melish lost his church and thus his livelihood, he went to work for the Southern Conference Education Fund. Traveling in the South to raise money, he met some of the remarkable people the civil rights movement was producing. Many of them came north to speak and often they stayed in the house where Angela was living. No one would have called her an activist at that point, but Reverend Melish recalls her admiration for these new leaders, in whom she no doubt saw a new kind of awareness among blacks, one that called for decisive action. At the Melishes she encountered the Rev. Fred Shuttlesworth whose children she had known in Birmingham. Reverend Shuttlesworth and his wife were, in 1957, the first black people to attempt to enroll their children in Birmingham's public schools. Shuttlesworth was beaten with chains and brass knckles, his daughter and wife were stabbed and knocked around, while whites shouted, "Kill this nigger and it will be all over. Don't let him get away. Let's end it today."

Apart from politics, daily life for Angela was scheduled so tightly with activities that Mrs. Melish finally wrote to Mrs. Davis, asking permission for Angela to discontinue her piano lessons. She had a room of her own, where, after school, she studied late into the evening and practiced her clarinet. Often after coming home from school with the Melish boys, she stopped for a cup of tea and a bit of gossip with Aunt Ella, an invalid relative who lived with the family and had tea waiting every day for Angela, whom she adored. If it was lonely away from home at times, there was much to do. Given her first taste of independence, Angela occasionally stayed out overnight at a girlfriend's house, and there were few restrictions about where she went or what she did. The Melishes never sheltered their children from what was happening and illusions rarely got inside the front door.

It was probably just as well that Angela was learning to deal with things at home in Brooklyn. What she came up against in high school was difficult enough. So much was happening at once, new experiences were piling up; and the intensely academic, highly political, and largely white high school wasn't an easy place to survive in. At Elisabeth Irwin High School things were perhaps often tough enough—in subtle ways—to have sent another girl home for good.

5/HIGH SCHOOL AND PICKET LINES

"Mary had a little lamb, its fleece was white as snow,
And everywhere that Mary went her lamb was sure to go.
Now Mary had another lamb, its fleece was very black,
And everywhere that Mary went that lamb was turned
    right back."

"One, two, three, four,
Don't go into Woolworth's Store."

Greenwich Village was the center of our world when I was in high school. There was Washington Square, where you could meet up with your friends on a Sunday afternoon. There were the coffeehouses along Macdougal Street where we hung out after school. We went to the movies at the Waverly, played ball in the courts on Third Street, browsed in the paperback bookstores that had just begun to flourish. At the center of the center was Eighth Street, and where it converged with Sixth Avenue, a Howard Johnson's restaurant. It's where I most clearly remember sitting and talking with Angela, endlessly puffing at cigarettes. Most of what we said was profoundly unmemorable. It was the small exchange of adolescent female chatter—boys, smoking, parents, movies—but after a number of these unremarkable conversations and the consumption of numerous mocha frosties, rare cheeseburgers, fried clams, cherry Cokes, and gallons of coffee, we seemed to know each other well enough for me to ask the difficult question: What was it like to be black and grow up in the South? Angela laughed about the debutantes and the swimming pools, but she said little about the bombings and she never told melodramatic stories about dogs and firehoses. I've sometimes wondered why.

Was she playing a role for her white-middle-class friends?

Cattycornered from Howard Johnson's, on Greenwich Avenue where it veers west toward Seventh Avenue, there is a ugly decaying fortress-like building. Slits for windows covered with bars, the Women's House of Detention brooded in our backyard. We were a little afraid of the women who screamed out from behind those bars. None of us ever thought too much about what might go on inside.

When Angela was arrested in October of 1970, she was taken to the Women's House of Detention. It was growing chilly, but the constant stream of protesters crowded outside. Angela was inside.

Later, when I saw her in her cell at San Rafael, she gave me an account of those days in New York, part of an unpublished manuscript:

> . . . I learned the screeching sirens and unending caravan were heading in the direction of Sixth Avenue and Greenwich Avenue: the Women's House of Detention. Shame overcame me—not, of course, because I was about to be jailed but rather because before now I had never seriously thought about my sisters inside this very familiar building. I am referring concretely to this specific building. During the last two years of my high school days, I spent much of my time in the area surrounding the House of Detention. The high school was a few blocks away and in my daily trips to and from the subway and to other places in Greenwich Village, I'd see this monstrous structure, frequently catching the women-screams bellowing through the windows. It bothered me, I recall! I was often afraid to look up, being too inhibited to scream back myself. This medieval dungeon of screaming women would disturb me, but its own stone impenetrability always left me trying

to ignore the effect it was having on me. Now I was joining the women of ten years ago—perhaps if I made a great effort, I would be excused for my earlier studied apathy.

In the dark and dirty room where I spent the next few hours I glanced at the bulletin board and caught a glimpse for the very first time of the now obsolete FBI wanted poster. Noticing this, someone hastened to take it down. I'll never know whether this gesture was conceived in concern or was meant to exude satisfaction about the way "law and order" had prevailed. But next to the newly vacant space on the board, there was yet another poster depicting yet another woman sought by J. Edgar Hoover's troops. Uncanny this convergence of circumstances: this woman had been one of my twenty-five classmates in the high school a few blocks away.

A ten-minute walk south from the Women's House of Detention brings you to Charlton Street at the south end of Greenwich Village. Elisabeth Irwin High School squats at No. 40, an uninspired structure as wide as it is tall, with a façade that gives no suggestion of the casual, colorful disarray inside.

It was the "beatnik era" when Angela first arrived at E.I., escorted each day by the older Melish boys until she learned the complications of the New York subway system well enough to go it alone. She was amazed to see teachers in jeans and beards, students in pants and long hair. Little things struck her—you could wear what you liked, could smoke and call teachers by their first names; they treated you differently too. The teachers at E.I. had no use for the authoritarian methods she was accustomed to.

Angela and I were not in the same class—she was a year ahead of me—but with no more than two hundred pupils in the whole school sooner or later everyone knew everyone else. By the time I got to know her she was taking the "beatniks" in her stride; though rather earnest and serious, she seemed to fit in as though she had never been to any other school.

Elisabeth Irwin was also a terrific challenge not only to her mind but to her emotions. It was the first time she had gone to an integrated school (*i.e.*, largely white). And because of the poor schools for blacks which the South had created, she was forced to work hard just to get by. Angela never intended merely to get by; she was determined to succeed and to excel. The habit of being first in school was hard to lose. The pressures to succeed were enormous. She had come a long way for this education and she owed it to her family to get it. To comply with the school rules for all transferees, Angela was forced to repeat her junior year. She'd had little math and science and no languages in Birmingham. Requirements for "good" Northern colleges were rigid: four years of languages, four of math and science, social studies, English. There were no exceptions for potentially bright black students. The only thing to do was to work like hell.

Much has been made of the fact that Angela's worst subject was French but that by gritting her teeth and buckling down to it, she made it her best subject by the time she finished high school. The truth was really much simpler. A beginner in French, she had to learn in two years what the others got in four. The way Angela tells it, she did what she had to, discovering in herself a formidable ability to cope despite her deeper uncertainties and fears.

Obsessed, determined, or matter-of-fact, Angela set off in pursuit of French, and, helped by special tutoring, eventually acquired an excellent command of the language. The level of French studies, like everything else at Elisabeth

Irwin, was high. A summer course at Tours or Pau or Grenoble was encouraged, a status symbol as well as an opportunity to master colloquial French. The students chattered with each other in French and crossed their sevens. Malraux, Gide, Sartre, but especially Camus were senior-year staples.

Elisabeth Irwin High School was an outgrowth of the Little Red School House. Little Red had begun as an elementary-level experiment in the public-school system in the 1930s—a test case for progressive education—but the system recognized it for the foreign body it was and rejected it violently. Before the Second World War, Little Red turned private. E.I. was founded to supply progressive education at the point where Little Red left off. It was probably as radical a school as existed. Many of the teachers had been forced out of other jobs during the McCarthy era and E.I. displayed an extraordinary decency toward them. The same was often true of the parents. The school has with age and a change of staff become less and less sympathetic to radical causes, but in the early 1960s social conscience and political awareness were integral to its life. Political involvement expressed itself in classroom discussion, in demonstrations, and in lighter-hearted ways: during air-raid drills students gathered in the cafeteria and sang "Down by the Riverside" ("Ain't Gonna Study War No More") and refused to take shelter or crawl under the desks. It sounds trivial, but it wasn't: not to comply with air-raid-drill rules was illegal.

To meet the intellectual demands made by the school, students read Dostoevsky, Pirandello, T. S. Eliot, and discussed Marxism. Discussion was encouraged. Angela sat quietly in class, taking notes, absorbing everything she heard, but rarely talking up. Teachers remember an extremely reticent person. The written word was considered as important as talk. Scores of essays, stories, and poems passed across the English teacher's desk. Music, art, and drama were not only emphasized but required. Even the tone-deaf had to sing in Chorus. There were the class trips, coordinated with a given year's field of study. Students who had never seen the country found themselves milking cows on farms, reading Thoreau at Walden Pond and Hawthorne in Salem. The junior class would be dispatched to some place like Mahanoy City in Pennsylvania's coal-mining territory to see American Economic History translated into industrial bricks and mortar and into the workshirted lives people led, so different from their own New York existence.

Elisabeth Irwin, however, for all its progressive nature and its liberal outlook, was fiercely competitive. Angela first met tough intellectual competition at E.I., and it left its mark. The insistence on high standards pressured students to do well. Angela's class was among the first lot of war babies. The explosion of applicants for college was dangled constantly before our brains at E.I. Competition was intense in much subtler ways too. For a progressive school that had a deep radical streak, there was a complicated social life that relied on status in a variety of shades. There were parties and dances and clothes and gossip. No one was concerned with these things the way "other" high-school students were. No one wore a circle pin or a bunny-fur jacket. We did, however, stride to and from school in our English trenchcoats. Style was important—very important—and it covered what you wore, saw, did, and read (Camus, William Golding) as well as what you listened to (Pete Seeger, Miles Davis). A change came in Angela's last year. Rock 'n' roll burst onto the scene and the school shed its disdain for Elvis Presley and the teenybopper. At noon in the senior room (juniors and seniors could *smoke* here at lunchtime) everyone learned the Twist while the formerly "straight" math genius sang a current hit called "Mother-in-Law."

The students were pretty sophisticated sexually for 1960, or at least tried to pass as such. They knew their way around New York. Those who dominated were highly political, intensely academic, or very hip, and often all three. They were an awesome lot to face. Tough, intellectual, cynical, and with-it, as only a certain breed of middle-class New Yorkers who think of themselves and their world as the exact center of the universe can be.

It wasn't pleasant to be an outsider at Elisabeth Irwin. Most of the students had known each other from the age of three or four. The parents all knew each other too, and it was the parents who were in command. They played a large part and they paid a great deal: in 1960 tuition was about $1400 per child annually, except for those students like Angela who had scholarships. The arrangement worked well inasmuch as the administration never got a chance to become autocratic: the parents checked it. Teachers and parents knew each other well and many spent summers in the same Vermont town. But as a result of all this togetherness the atmosphere at E.I. was very inbred. Liberal, predominantly Jewish, well-to-do, the parents were mostly professionals or connected with the arts. The number of Republican and/or suburban families was tiny. There would have been more, for it was a hard time to get your kids into a good high school and E.I. was academically superb, but the conservative and especially the nouveau riche (if it showed) were excluded from the parental power structure. They were made miserably aware of their difference, of the fact that E.I. did not mean to open its arms to women who wore their minks to school meetings. As for black parents, there were so few it hardly mattered.

Angela sensed some of this, though basically she had come to E.I. for an education, not to conduct a critique on the New York middle classes. She was still too young, too unradical, too unanalytic to see the rat-race implications of this liberal, progressive school; she was by intellectual endowment cut out for academic distinction and happy in acquiring it. There were times, however, when she had an inkling of what was going on, an unarticulated sense that came largely from her dealings with her friends' parents.

Some of the teachers and parents really did reach out to try for change. Mrs. Melish, with three boys at E.I., was committed to revising the social setup at the school, and she and others, working with the American Friends committee whose program had brought Angela north, set up interracial groups to study the prospects. Mrs. Melish recalls meetings at which parents prodded each other to face up to their own attitudes. Black parents told of the humiliations they suffered; a few white parents responded. The trouble was that those who bothered were already committed. Just as there were a few parents who cared, there were a few students who approached Angela on a strictly personal level. Angela remains close today to the few good friends she made at E.I.

But for the most part the parents, as white liberal New Yorkers, were faced with a problem in Angela (and a few others) which they were at a loss to solve: she fitted none of their stereotypes. This was the core of the subtle antagonisms she occasionally felt. Indoctrinated by birth and education, or by their identity as good white Northern and New York liberals, the parents (and often their children) held notions about the South and black people that were not only fanciful and provincial but plainly prejudiced. The South was far away, a jungle of poverty and hatred inhabited by novelists, sheriffs, red-necked whites, and poor black people who were just waiting for Northern whites to descend on them with schemes for a better life. It was so easy, so satisfying to help out those disadvantaged black people down there. Well spoken, well bred, well dressed, and from a solidly middle-class family, Angela was different. She posed a subtle menace. She was, after all, as bright, as well off, as happy, even as clean as their own children. And she came by it naturally, just as they did. At first parents praised themselves for their own children's liberal activities, and if cultivating Angela was one, all the better. Angela slept over at their houses, picketed Woolworth's with their children, partied and went to school with them.

It wasn't wholly conscious, but the more the parents saw of Angela, and the few others like her, the more they saw she was much more real than they had imagined. They liked her, they approved of her, she was one of them. Yet in some unexpressed way they realized that her attitudes differed from their own. That, too, was okay. Up to a point. But having identified her as black, they saw that they couldn't treat her the way they had treated most other black people. It left them groping for an attitude toward this new phenomenon. There was no need to sympathize with Angela, no way to work for her or raise funds in her cause. She was right there in their homes, their neighborhood, their school. She was there because their own school had invited her to come. It was impossible to send her away once the benefit party ended.

A few people completely disregarded Angela's color, and made the assumption that she was "just like them." A lot of them simply averted their eyes, almost as if embarrassed to confess that they really knew that her skin was a different color from their own. Years later Angela recalled the feelings she could not express at E.I. Able now to define her reactions, she says she felt her blackness more than she ever had in the South—not in the customary racist ways, but because people made such effusive overtures to her and because of their awkward attempts to ignore that she was black. An undercurrent of anger was there too, growing from her un-

certainty about white friendliness. She noticed that a lot of
white people felt that they had to make special efforts—to
talk to her, to invite her home for dinner—because she was
black and from the South. Angela began to erect screens to
protect herself from an alien world; screens also allowed her
to adapt to that world, to play the role she had to in order to
survive. She could not rebel the way her white classmates
could and did: as one of the privileged few she owed too
much to her parents and her race to give up her determination to succeed. Angela, unlike most of her friends at E.I.,
had also at an early age dealt with a certain kind of reality.

There was at E.I., especially among the parents, an ele-
ment of fear. Prosperity was newfound, insecurity a constant
emotional threat. Moreover, many of the parents had been
Communists, or fellow-travelers, some had been investigated
during the McCarthy era, and in reaction they gave up politics and dug deep into their lives at home. People built a
comfy, uncommitted private life to protect their children, to
save them from "what we've been through" (the Depression,
the war, the McCarthy era). The children rebelled against
this fear, lashing out at their parents' silence. You could draw
a parallel between Angela and her family and the E.I. students and theirs: roots in radicalism, work in civil rights;
children who turned militant and became the SDS members
or Weathermen or Black Panthers of the late 1960s. Except
that Angela knew she would have to work for herself and her
people. Her white friends were stranded: there was "nothing" to do for themselves and their ideas were often abstract.
Action seemed something you undertook only for the blacks.
It was condescending, but nobody knew it then.

If Angela felt disoriented at Elisabeth Irwin, living
away from home and among white people for the first time
in her life, she also managed to enjoy herself and to learn a
great deal. One classmate who knew her well remembers her

primarily as a "great girl to roll in the grass in Central Park with." Angela dated boys in her class occasionally, but like others in the school, she more often went out in a group—to a picnic on Staten Island, to parties, to a jazz club in Greenwich Village. She was not part of the "promiscuous set." Apart from these outings with school friends, there were activities outside the school where Angela functioned on her own. These were times she could leave behind the inevitable label of the school's prize black pupil.

As part of the social studies program everyone at E.I. was required to spend a few hours each week at a local settlement house, acquiring "social consciousness." At the Brooklyn Heights Youth Center, which Mrs. Melish had a hand in running, the Melishes were surprised to see how easily Angela dealt with the tough kids who used it. And she was surprised at their surprise. "I knew kids like that all my life. Of course I knew how to talk to them." Working with the black teen-agers at the center may have become an escape from new pressures into something resembling the familiar. Angela spent hours with the kids from the Brooklyn gangs: the Outside Pharaohs, the Inside Pharaohs, the Ambassadors, the Apaches, and their girlfriends. It was a place to meet, to get in from the cold, to talk. Angela and Flo Mason, a friend from E.I., were determined at first to produce plays, but found themselves giving reading lessons instead. The lessons weren't much of a success. Everyone preferred talking. Some kids had never really talked to anyone in their lives, but they talked to Angela, pouring out the frustrations of being black and young, of the city, drugs, parents. With her usual self-deprecation Angela says, "I didn't go there because I felt I had any special skills, but much more because I enjoyed the atmosphere and could identify with the problems which came up." A young man, though, told Mrs. Melish privately that Angela was the only person in his whole life he ever told the truth to. Somehow she got herself across. People responded.

She found another release from the tensions that were building at Elisabeth Irwin when she discovered politics. As her last year approached and she felt more and more the impossibility of going home for good, she began to wonder about the future. Trips home were frustrating, as the gulf widened between her new ideas and those of her parents, old friends, relatives. But she was no more at home among the white liberals in New York. She was beginning to need a substitute family, a place to belong. The longing for involvement, hidden, deep, rarely mentioned, was growing.

"Two, four, six, eight, Woolworth's doesn't integrate," came the cries every Saturday morning. Angela was there, chanting with the rest of us in the frosty winter day. Picketing Woolworth's regularly was an unofficial requirement at E.I. Teachers, students, even the occasional parent showed up to join in. Chanting slogans, admonishing shoppers not to enter Woolworth's doors, the straggly line with its gaily painted signs circled eagerly in front of the store. Between ten and noon those Saturdays, Thirty-ninth Street and Fifth Avenue were full of our civil rights songs and calls of "Don't go into Woolworth's. Please don't shop in Woolworth's." The mornings ended with hot chocolate at a coffee shop on Thirty-ninth Street where long conversations about civil rights—and less pressing problems—lasted well into the afternoon.

It was an exciting time. When the first black students in the South began walking downtown and sitting at lunch counters and demanding service, a new era had begun. All kinds of possibility for change opened up. The newspapers and television reports were full of it and of the terrors of police reprisal. White students in the North adopted the techniques their Southern counterparts were evolving. Police brutality became a reality for us when during a rally in Times Square a cop on a horse grabbed one of my classmates and dragged him three blocks. Nonviolence was inviolable. Everyone joined the NAACP and SANE (The Committee for a Sane Nuclear Policy), naïvely certain that the world could be changed by protest in the streets. All you had to do was learn the slogans, sign petitions, paint signs, and most of all go to rallies together. Standing there singing "We Shall Overcome" we felt ecstatic.

Angela's commitment reflected the general level of political sophistication. Some who knew her at high school argue that there was nothing of the activist about her then, and that her later political involvement was due to a blinding flash of revelation that struck her in Germany when she was twenty-two. Others claim that she was always a completely political person, even as a seventeen-year-old student at E.I. Neither of these interpretations really fits.

To those with firm middle-class civil rights attitudes, she seemed nonpolitical because her commitment was not what they thought it ought to be. In fact, she was feeling her way, and it simply wasn't very clear where it would lead her. She did what there was to do—picketed Woolworth's, went on peace marches, worked at the community center. This was the level of political activity that existed in 1961 for someone determined to continue with and succeed in academic work. Her thinking began to change radically, though, and two families—the Melishes and the Apthekers—were influential. From the Melishes she drew a sense of what political involvement meant in practical terms. She learned how heavy the price might be. From Herbert Aptheker she began to learn about ideas, absorbing, if only by osmosis, socialist theory and economic history, during the evenings she and Aptheker's daughter, Bettina, painted signs.

Dr. Aptheker, Director of the American Institute for

Marxist Studies, has long been one of the leading theoreticians of America's leftist radicals. Himself Jewish and white, he is considered the foremost scholar of Black American History, a mantle he inherited from W.E.B. DuBois along with a whole collection of the famous black historian's private papers. He has written DuBois' biography, as well as many other books, which in 1953 were removed by the State Department from its overseas libraries. He now teaches at Bryn Mawr College.

Bettina Aptheker was in 1960 a member of the Communist Party's Youth Commission and also ran a Marxist youth group called Advance. From the age of seventeen, when she got her ribs cracked in a demonstration in New York, she has taken part in almost every major Left-wing march and has twice been jailed, most recently for her part in the Berkeley Free Speech Movement of 1965, which she helped organize. Bettina later became one of the central figures in the national defense campaign to free Angela from jail.

In Bettina's Advance were the sons and daughters of black Left-wingers, friends of Mrs. Davis, whom Angela had earlier met on summer visits to New York or grown up with in Birmingham. Among them was Margaret Burnham, the daughter of activists Louis and Margaret Burnham who were close to the Davises in Birmingham. They had moved to New York. Angela and Margaret renewed their friendship, and the two stayed close throughout Angela's New York years. Margaret went on to become a very skillful lawyer. Years later, in 1972, she used those skills to defend her childhood friend Angela. Angela not only worked with Margaret and other young blacks in Advance; she was very close to them, perhaps placing a special value on her black friends in the so largely white world of New York. Now a New Yorker herself, Angela collaborated actively with

these militant youngsters, and in this work her old sentimental attachment to the Party was reawakened and developed. She found too in Advance a first taste of the kind of
solidarity political groups provide: the feeling of complete
togetherness with others.

E.I. encouraged political activity—it was almost part of
the syllabus—and those who wouldn't march, who wouldn't
picket were regarded with some disdain. The excitement
mounted during Angela's last year, with weekly picketing.
There were increasingly frequent rallies and marches. The
Freedom Rides began. At E.I. the principal gave advice
on how to behave if arrested and what to do if the police
harassed you. There were anti-air-raid-shelter protests, anti-
bomb marches, benefit dances for the NAACP. Angela was
no more or less a part of this than most students. She was
not sufficiently involved to go on Freedom Rides, but she
cared enough to work hard in Advance and the NAACP.

Toward Angela's last spring in high school there was
a long march. It was Easter 1961 and it was cold and very
wet. Early in the morning hundreds, then thousands of people began to show up under the George Washington Bridge.
Everyone had a daffodil, bright-yellow symbols of spring
and hope to wave against the dismal sodden sky. We began,
slowly at first, to walk downtown. More and more people
joined. We walked faster, singing, chanting, holding up our
banners denouncing nuclear testing. Here was a cause with
none of the constraints of protests against racism. We were
all involved, there was no undercurrent of condescension,
and for a moment togetherness was more than an empty
term. Smiles burst through Angela's usually serious expression. She held her daffodil and waved it at friends. It rained
harder; we walked faster, pacing ourselves all the way to
Forty-second Street. We swung east, striding toward the
United Nations. As we went through an underpass everyone

began singing "We shall overcome—we shall not be moved."

Everyone sang, louder and louder, all the way to the United Nations Plaza, where we massed together, close enough to feel warmth from each other. There were speeches and we cried out the responses. Then there was cheering: Pete Seeger, who had just been indicted, had arrived. The crowds parted, making an aisle for him. He passed through us to the platform and began to sing. We sang too—soaking wet, out of tune. There seemed to be enough of us to move worlds.

Angela was graduated that June and her graduation was marked by laughter. Milton Galamison, a Brooklyn minister and civil rights leader, was the guest speaker. He finished a provocative speech calling the class of 1961 to action. He returned to his chair at the edge of the platform crowded with Angela's classmates—the girls in white dresses, the boys in unfamiliar dark suits. Angela saw it about to happen, but there was no way to stop it. Galamison's chair tipped back. Everything went flying—minister, chair, and table piled with diplomas—and disappeared backstage behind the blue velvet curtain. After the laughter the ceremonies resumed. Angela got her diploma. High school was over.

6/BRANDEIS: A LIBERAL EDUCATION

"Intellectual inconoclasm was at the heart of the school's existence."

—INGRID BENGIS

Waltham, Massachusetts, is one of the anonymous suburbs that scatter out endlessly around Boston. Far enough from the city to lose much real connection with it—cultural or otherwise—Brandeis University seems to turn in on itself. The campus has an almost inhospitable air. A series of steep hills looks out over a pretty stretch of New England countryside, but the university has little in common with it. Littering the hills, almost as if at random, are the stark modern buildings—each with the name of a famous donor carved over the entry—resembling nothing so much as the wings and pavilions of a large hospital. The only and startling exception is an old "castle" (a reminder that the campus was once the estate of a country house) surrounded by low well-worn stone walls and crawling with ivy. Angela lived here as a senior.

". . . Brandeis doesn't start until the 21st. As school draws nearer, I am beginning to have mixed feelings. I am certainly looking forward to it, but in other ways I'm a little apprehensive," Angela wrote to me late in August of 1961 from Los Angeles.

She was spending the summer with her wealthy aunt, and she was having a ball. Nothing could have been a greater contrast to the earnest politics of Advance or the excitement of protest demonstrations than the *dolce vita*

Angela was enjoying in opulent California. Like any other New York teen-ager rocketed suddenly into a world of movie stars and make-believe, she couldn't get over her good luck. Her letters reflect how starry-eyed she was. "My aunt has this fabulous house," wrote the future preacher of equality; "twenty-five rooms with a swimming pool and waterfalls and it's real groovy." She told me that a cousin was taking her, by foreign sports car, to the nightclubs on Sunset Strip, that she was staying up far too late, that she was off to tour Mexico, that she filled in idle moments practicing French on her aunt's gardener: "She has a French gardener who won't talk to me in anything but French." But she was also careful to explain that this plutocratic paradise—so unlikely a feature in her background—was all the result of her aunt's involvement in real estate. Finding herself in a more fluid society than she had ever known, Angela must have felt intoxicated by the greater freedom. But what her letters to me over that month really show is the lightheartedness of any girl in her position, on vacation from politics, academic competition, racial tension.

When her summer romance with California was over, she spent a week in New York with the Melishes en route to college. It was with encouragement from Reverend Melish that she had chosen Brandeis, although her mother, eager for the best for a brilliant daughter, favored Ivy League Mount Holyoke. Angela, however, disliked the slightly prissy flavor of Mount Holyoke left over from its days as a missionary school.

When Brandeis offered her a full scholarship, Mr. Davis, a practical man with three more children to educate, urged her to accept. She did, and just before the school year began Reverend Melish drove Angela to Waltham, delivering her—books, clothes, and the apprehensions she had felt during the summer—to Brandeis.

If the campus was architecturally stark and the winters cold, the intellectual atmosphere of the university was overcharged. It was progressive well beyond its era. Intellectual intensity, a high level of competitiveness and radical fervor sparked high-powered and often emotional discussion. People like Abbie Hoffman and several Weathermen were products of Brandeis in the early 1960s. The teaching was superb and graduates often displayed a dazzling brilliance in their careers. Feelings ran high on almost every subject: students continually dissected their own and everyone else's motives as if in a giant lab where they used themselves and their friends as specimens. Intellectualism was the brain of Brandeis, its political radicalism the guts. The style was beat. Ingrid Bengis, a classmate of Angela's, writes, "intellectual iconoclasm was at the heart of the school's existence (the most popular courses were the Sociology of Terror; the Intellectual History of Europe; Dostoevsky, Gide, and Mann; and Marcuse's lectures on Modern Political Theory). Young minds, alienated sensibilities and revolutionary ideas were bound to produce an explosive mix, which, even if it didn't go off right away, would reverberate down the corridors of the 60s." She adds, "There was a split at Brandeis. There were the socialites and the rebels and it was war. You could sit right next to some guy and feel totally alienated from him and know that the only thing that bound you together was that you were all alienated."

At first Angela too felt alienated at Brandeis. She felt isolated and cut off from Birmingham, even from New York, where she had come to feel at home, and from herself. She also discovered at that time that out of fifteen hundred students she was one of about ten blacks. It wasn't yet time when you necessarily went out of your way to make friends with the black girl at school. If you did, you pretended not to notice she was any different at all. But over the first weeks

Angela realized, perhaps with resignation as well as relief, that Brandeis was basically a continuation of what Elisabeth Irwin had been; there was the same elitist-progressive mix but with a leavening of foreign students. As entering freshmen her class was given Allen Ginsburg's "Howl" and Robert Lowell's *Life Studies* to read during orientation week.

Despite her feelings of loneliness and the conflicts gestating inside her, Angela functioned very well. She settled in and turned her energies full force toward academic success.

She chose French as a major, largely because she wanted to go to France, and she excelled at it. She was extremely quiet, serious, and hardworking, her adviser, Professor Murray Sachs, recalls. A rather gentle, liberal man, he confesses he hardly knew her, largely because he rarely became involved with his students as individuals. She seemed, as he remembers her, to know a number of people, but never to be close to anyone, and he thought her extraordinarily reserved. Professor Sachs never once saw her personal feelings show themselves in public. It may be that she needed, almost waited for, someone to trust enough with her feelings, and that Sachs's reluctance to "pry" only encouraged her emotional isolation. However this may be, she carried herself with great dignity and had, Sachs felt, a deep sense of her own worth—which came not from breaking out of a ghetto, not from being beaten down and proving she could get up, but from the fact that she had been brought up to believe in herself. No doubt the face Angela presented to her adviser and to Brandeis was carefully arranged: she never showed signs of being hung up about being black. True, Brandeis provided as hospitable an atmosphere as any. It was not closed in any painful way to Angela: she was not subjected to a racist society there, though, as at high school, whites tended to be oversolicitous.

In her work she gave a "solid performance, but little of herself," according to Professor Sachs. He saw in her a capacity for hard work rather than brilliant creativity. Her ability and willingness to persevere and her self-discipline struck him. Throughout her time at college her performance was excellent, and her comprehensive exams were as good as the best if not better. She had, Sachs says, middle-class values in education.

Lannie Goldberg, an outgoing, flamboyant New Yorker from the plush suburb of Scarsdale, was Angela's closest friend, and it was she who pulled Angela from the shyness, the reserve, and the loneliness in which she lived just down the corridor. Ingrid Bengis, the third member of the little group that formed and clung together, describes how Angela first opened up: "When I first knew Angie, she hardly ever smiled. But gradually she acquired a sort of skittish laugh which popped out at unexpected moments and then retreated as if she weren't sure she could take a chance on really laughing. In our more lightheaded moments, the three of us took to speaking a language of our own invention, a cross between baby talk and pig Latin, and each evening we could be seen walking to the dining room together, gibbering away: Angela tall, dignified, reserved, Lannie bouncing along in her bare feet, tossing her long black hair insolently, I tagging along behind, somewhat unsure of my place in the triumvirate." They were all seventeen then, ready and willing to try on rebellions for size and find one that fit, prepared to accept student disenchantment as a standard part of college experience.

But while Ingrid and Lannie could go for broke in yanking themselves out by the roots—the roots that went deep into their middle-class background, parents, the suburban lives they had come from and had come to despise—it wasn't so easy for Angela. Who was there at all-white all-middle-class Brandeis for Angela to emulate? The others could discharge their anger into a "cultural revolution," identify with the beats, and find security in a new lifestyle, a home away from home in the land where rebellion was already a comfortably established mode. For Angela "it was quite another thing to turn on your parents when their struggle was part of the as yet almost unbegun struggle for the freedom of a still oppressed class." Angry outrage and the feeling of betrayal upon discovering that one's parents did not practice the values they espoused was enough for Lannie and Ingrid, but not for Angela, who seemed as yet too fixed on the idea of academic success to turn away from it, and who simply knew that in the longer range of rebellion she and her parents would be on the same side.

"Cultivation" is the word which for Ingrid conjures up the images of the Angela she knew. Cultivated, nicely brought up to study hard and to succeed. But she was never "bourgeois" in the sense of valuing wealth and status. She could play the "cultivated" role, says Ingrid; it was a kind of screen she set up, a means of coping with the world around her, a screen behind which a lot of anger, even a deep rage was hidden. She let her friends know that her parents' way of life wasn't hers: committed to civil rights though they might be, the Davis parents were also too committed to piano lessons and everything they symbolized for Angela's liking. She didn't break with them, didn't even make her disagreements too clear. That Angela didn't break with her parents perhaps indicates an instinctive political knowledge that being black undercut most other things. Then too, Angela had not found another "home" or another world to which she belonged. She was very sensitive and very intense—a person of extraordinary feeling—but very well-defended also. Ingrid believes that "cultivation" was a persona Angela presented to the world.

Despite her outward success, Angela felt she was in some ways "marking time," almost wasting her life. The world seemed flat, tasteless, and stale. There was no sense of destiny, yet she retained a feeling that it was necessary to live by principle. The summer after her freshman year she went abroad. The people she met provided an exhilarating moment in which perhaps the conscious political being in her was born.

In Paris for a couple of months of study at the Alliance Française, she met young Algerian rebels and heard stories of their struggles, for at this time Algeria was still part of France and fighting for its independence. There were killings and assassinations and people told her she mustn't go out at night—she might be mistaken for an Algerian. Her meetings with the rebels gave her an insight into a situation from which she drew parallels about her own people. She felt a bond between herself and the Algerians she met, and the beginnings of a desire to involve herself in some kind of revolution, some kind of effort to improve the world. It was to be several years before she did commit herself, however, and then it was to a cause more familiar to her than a foreign liberation struggle.

That same summer of 1962 she met up with the Cuban Revolution and came away excited. It was a vivid episode, so alive that the memory came to her in very precise detail some ten years later in the jail cell at Marin: "There is an unchanging paucity about the outer circumstances of imprisonment, particularly if you are held in quasi-solitary confinement. Long-term prisoners probably have, as a rule, a larger storehouse of memories than most. Conceivably they also have more elaborate dreams. These subjective events seem to spontaneously arise as compensations, more or less, for objective emptiness. Not long ago, an experience unfortunately forgotten somewhere in the ten years since its occurrence suddenly, and without any apparent external stimulus, vividly penetrated my field of consciousness: my first direct contact with the Cuban Revolution. After surviving my freshman year in college I attended the International Youth Festival of Peace and Friendship in Helsinki."

The young Cubans invited the American delegates to a cultural show at their headquarters. Angela was astonished at the revolutionary enthusiasm and especially the commitment of the young Cubans to building their country. Everyone else, she remembers, was enthralled with the show, for they saw art and revolution combining for the first time in one event. As the evening ended everyone in the hall linked arms and danced out through the doors into the streets of Helsinki. The Finns were amazed at the sight of a few hundred people singing and dancing down the middle of the road. "But such was the impact of the Cubans' revolutionary spirit on us."

Helsinki also gave Angela her first taste of tear gas, when a confrontation between festival members and some "Hell's Angels types" brought out the police. She came home after that and there were telephone calls and unannounced visits from the FBI, exceedingly curious to know just why she had attended a "Communist" gathering and what she had done there.

After the excitement of the summer Angela began her second year at Brandeis. All her passion was slowly channeled into philosophy. In the philosophical interpretation of literature, she felt, one might come to grips with what human beings were all about. "Literature and philosophy are enlaced in my own vision," she says. She read Proust, all the hundreds of pages of *A La recherche du temps perdu*, and she read Schopenhauer and Bergson and Nietzsche, seeking ideas that might explain the world to her and from which she could form a pattern to impose upon her own life.

For Angela philosophy wasn't a question of sophomore bull sessions on the state of the universe and neither had it anything to do with acquiring academic apparatus, Ingrid Bengis notes. It was a tremendous passion, a way in which to deal with the hardest problems of human beings, their nature, their spirit. But there was another spur to her awakening interest in philosophy: a West German exchange student named Manfred Clemenz. Angela rarely talked about boys and when she talked of Manfred Clemenz, it was always in terms of the philosophic ideas he broached. She never discussed their personal relationship until, to Ingrid's astonishment, "Suddenly she announced she was going to marry him." Angela says she made no such statement.

In spite of Angela's reticence, which was so striking a feature of her character, she did occasionally break down and let her closest friends into her secrets. In an article in the *Village Voice* Ingrid relates how shattered Lannie Goldberg was when Angela let her know that someone, some time in the South had seriously frightened her. "She doesn't trust boys at all," Lannie reported; "she thinks most of them are pretty much like those guys in the South. . . . And her parents don't know a thing." Angela's friends marveled at her matter-of-fact way of telling "Southern horror stories"; it was as if, they said, "all her emotions had been buried inside of her and nothing external could touch her any more."

This picture of Angela—friendly on the surface, reserved if you tried to dig beneath it—is the Angela I knew the year before in New York, although to me she had never shown signs of trauma over boys. To me she seemed comfortable and open in her friendship with boys, but admittedly these friendships were of a casual high-school type that no one would have found very scary. I went to Brandeis myself in October of 1961 to be interviewed, and Angela seemed just as I had always known her—but more relaxed, more easygoing, perhaps because Brandeis was more open than E.I., less of a hothouse or, perhaps, simply bigger. Lannie and Ingrid, however, had seen that Angela was changing. Her rigid self-control and her Christian habit of turning the other cheek were giving way, just occasionally, to honest outbursts of anger.

Manfred Clemenz, a philosophy graduate from Frankfurt, represented, no doubt, part of a larger change in Angela. But how, after her earlier difficulties with boys, did she come to trust him? Obviously there was the appeal of his intellect, and he was a personable young man anyway, with his mustache and beard. But it is also possible that only in a framework of remote philosophic abstraction did Angela feel it safe to embark on a deep human relationship. It was certainly on an intellectual level that Manfred first approached her. At all events, when this young German came into her life, she didn't hesitate to commit herself. Lannie and Ingrid weren't the only ones taken by surprise.

Reverend Melish was at a civil liberties rally in New York in the spring of Angela's second year in college. Looking down from the platform, he watched the familiar scene, glancing here and there to catch the eye of friends in the crowd. Suddenly he saw Angela with a young man. She later introduced Manfred to the Reverend Melish, who says, "It is not my right or purpose to go into Angela's personal life, but correspondence in my possession indicates that Angela and Manfred had a serious interest in each other, and that both the families—the white German family in Frankfurt and the Davises in Birmingham—had their reservations. In fact, when Angela became interested in Manfred, Sallye Davis nearly popped her lid. But I said, 'Just ride it out, wait until Angela gets a taste of middle-class German life. Let her use her own good sense.' "

As her second year ended Angela continued to work very hard, but her horizons had expanded. Her contacts with Cuban and Algerian students had opened up the world a little and now she prepared with much anticipation to go to Paris for her junior year. But she was still living in a white world, and it wasn't until her last year at Brandeis that Angela became close to several black students, and also met Noel Day. Day was a black organizer in the Boston ghetto whom Angela got to know and who impressed her. Politically she remained inactive, waiting, it seemed, for the ripe moment to enter the political arena. It was as if she were biding her time until she knew exactly how to use herself and to what ends. She was "immensely impressed" when Malcolm X spoke at Brandeis, though she remembers completely misinterpreting the Muslims: put off by their black nationalist ethics and their attitude to women, she didn't recognize their role in politicizing the blacks. It was very difficult to acquire a "black consciousness as far as the autonomy of the black struggle was concerned, for all my experience until then had pointed the other way: black and white unite." She felt exhiliarated, however, "felt really good inside, surrounded by all the whites as I was" when Malcolm spoke.

A desire gradually emerged to exert her philosophical enthusiasms, to turn her strongest emotions outward instead of screening them off. Ingrid Bengis wrote, ". . . Sensitivity led her direcly to an intellectual understanding of her own condition, her dilemma as a black intellectual which in turn when combined with her passion led to a recognition of the inevitability of political revolt, of action which would break the dichotomy between her knowledge of how things were and her capacity to deal with that knowledge. For her growth became, in a way which it never became for us, a process of increasing self-division or reaching upward while having to keep her grip on everything behind her." When during sophomore year at Brandeis the Cuban missile crisis occurred, Ingrid remembers that "Angie was not so shocked . . . the missile crisis passed and I became depoliticized until the next crisis. Angela never did. Radicalism struck deep slow roots in her, I guess, because her 'Cuban missile crisis' had been with her for so long, since she was born in fact. It was so to speak in her blood."

". . . no matter where our fathers had been born, or what they had endured, the fact of Europe had formed us both, was part of our identity and part of our inheritance."

—James Baldwin

"Angela, elle trouve toujours le mot juste," Madame Lamotte was fond of saying. The Lamottes were Angela's "French family" during her junior year in France. Before she went to Paris and the Lamottes in autumn 1963, Angela stayed in Biarritz for six weeks of orientation. The other American students in the program were struck by her intelligence, her poise, and her sophistication. With her European experience of the summer before she already had a polish that made the others envious. One girl admitted that Angela was the only person she had met brighter than herself. Already Angela's French was excellent and outwardly she seemed to have great style, but she was never the sort of "Frenchie Poo" who goes to Paris primarily to acquire a good accent, some French clothes, and, if possible, a Frenchman. Among the students in Biarritz Angela made a few friends with whom she traveled to Paris in September. She made few other friends that year in France and rarely ventured much beyond them and her family in the Rue Duret.

Winding away from the Avenue Foch in Paris's fashionable Sixteenth Arrondissement, the Rue Duret is a narrow street of shops and old houses set in a nest of other small streets and easy to overlook: one can easily miss the Lamotte house. Shuttered family homes stand squashed between a pâtisserie, a pharmacie, and a confiserie, its window filled with marzipan animals, chocolate boxes sprouting pink ribbons, and branches of sugared almonds. You pass a small épicerie selling honey and health foods and English marmalade. There is a faint smell of spices. Just beyond it is number 27bis. The ancient stone building is unimposing.

Madame Lamotte is a large comfortable woman in a large and comfortable household. They suit each other. There is money, but there is nothing showy or snobbish about her. The apartment is big and with low ceilings; the furnishings are old and a bit worn, but very good. Rich rugs cover the floor. The rooms are a pleasant mélange of styles. Madame Lamotte, distinguished and kindly, speaks excellent English that, along with her penchant for good suits and sweaters, she inherited from an English grandmother.

Angela loved the food in France. (Everyone who knows her agrees she loves to eat.) She was, Madame Lamotte says, always curious about the French manner of eating— how to cut your cheese, how to conquer the challenge of peeling a pear at a single go. There was a strict rule at the Lamotte home: the girls who lived there (each year three Americans were put up) had to observe French customs at table. With the Lamottes, their five sons and a daughter, the Americans learned quickly.

There were two other girls that year, and because she didn't like one of them too well, Madame Lamotte felt unable to invite any of the trio to tea with the family or for evening visits. So she never got to know Angela as well as she would have liked. Angela moved into a big room with a girl named Christy Stagg on the floor below, where M. Lamotte's mother lived. The third girl, Jane Jordan, had a room with the Lamottes themselves. Jane felt that the Lamottes merely tolerated Angela, that she was okay because she was bright and pretty. But Angela thinks of the

Lamottes and her life in the Rue Duret with affection, and Madame Lamotte tells a story that shows clearly what she felt for Angela.

After her disappearance in the summer of 1970 the police called in to see if Madame Lamotte had recently heard from her. Madame Lamotte was out. When she came home and learned of the police interest, she sat down and, with French logic and thorough attention to detail, made a simple decision: if word came from Angela, she would keep it to herself. Although not political, Madame Lamotte is not uncynical about American justice, and if Angela should ever arrive in Paris, Madame Lamotte would simply take her in. There are children, friends, *femmes de ménage* in and out all day long. Amid the confusion of people and within the old-fashioned maze of rooms, Angela would very easily be absorbed. Madame Lamotte would be delighted to have her back in the Rue Duret.

"We sat around in cafés and talked most of the time," says Howard Block, another exchange student and Angela's best friend from that year abroad. Apart from Howard and a few others, Angela kept very much to herself. She was shy and withdrawn, uninterested in gathering large numbers of people about her. Howard, an intense and extremely articulate French scholar from Amherst, speaks with admiration and affection for her. Theirs was an easygoing, undemanding friendship. He was like a brother to her. The two were constant companions, living near each other and meeting every morning to board the Métro at Argentine and travel to classes together.

"We sat around in cafés and talked," Howard repeats. "And sometimes went rowing in the Bois de Boulogne—Angela liked that." There were endless walks around the city. Angela loved to walk, even ignoring her often swollen feet. There were lunches in cheap student restaurants in the

Latin Quarter. She especially liked couscous, a dish of which one can eat enormous quantities for a few francs. She browsed endlessly at the bookstalls, spending the little money she had. And in the evening there was more talk, usually at the Café de Sport near the Rue Duret rather than at the more trendy Left Bank hangouts. Occasional birthday parties called for excursions to the pâtisserie. A little bread and cheese and a lot of wine completed the celebrations. Howard describes Angela as "this combination of a shy blushy girl and someone who was also cynical and saw the real underbelly of things."

There were trips too—to Spain, to Sweden for Christmas, and to Germany. Howard and Angela hitched to Germany once. A middle-class fat German picked them up along the autobahn. Conniving to get Angela alone, he tried to dump Howard and continue on to Heidelberg. Howard staunchly refused to be dislodged. But the incident frightened Angela and offended her, as did the huge man who approached her one day in Paris: she and Howard were rushing down the Métro steps when a man loomed up in front of them and said he was an Israeli wrestler and wanted to take her home. She hurried away, annoyed and uneasy. "Everyone keeps talking about how men followed me all the time in Paris. But that's how it was for everyone—if you hung around in Left Bank cafés and stuff, that was just the kind of thing that happened," Angela explains, shrugging off any suggestion that she was unusually attractive to men.

There were few personal complications in Angela's life in Paris; her attitude was detached. She was outwardly self-contained, almost entirely self-sufficient in the life of the mind she led. She was involved deeply with no one except, of course, Manfred Clemenz, who had returned from Brandeis to Frankfurt and whom she occasionally visited. Unlike the Lamottes in Paris, Manfred Clemenz's parents in Germany did not welcome her. On her first visit to Frankfurt Angela was not made to feel too comfortable in the Clemenz house. Later, when Manfred had his own place, his landlady, Angela describes as "beautiful," made her feel at home. Howard Block found Manfred an extremely controlled, highly rational, intensely intellectual young man. Extremely interesting to talk to, Manfred was stimulating company, but Howard found him cool toward Angela and without apparent feeling or warmth, capable of making comments that seemed to Howard rather less than kind. Angela didn't talk to other people about her relationship with Manfred and always referred to him simply as her "friend."

"She put up a barrier between head and gut then, keeping things safely and delicately on an intellectual level," Howard remembers. She was plugged into the French intellectual scene—she read Sartre and other Existentialists, seeming more intrigued by their abstract theory than their activist committed works. (Six years later, when Angela gave the first lecture of her course on Existentialism at UCLA, she began by saying, "Man surges up in the world and defines himself," and continued in an intensely activist vein.) Her approach to her studies seemed to others an obsession rather than work toward an end or even a pleasure in itself. She did far more than her course required, perhaps nagged by her sense of privilege at being in Paris at all. She liked being in Paris, loved the language and the literature. She didn't like being privileged. Her determination to succeed, which had first appeared at Elisabeth Irwin, showed itself once more, but magnified. She took a course on the theater, she read late into the night, straining her eyes. But she seemed, in Howard Block's words, "to have put on the clutch between herself and what went on around her." Even in her choice of imaginative literature, she appeared to reject emotional involvement, choosing writers such as the highly abstract Alain Robbe-Grillet, the postwar French "new novelist," who abandons preoccupation with plot and character in his books to focus on man's relation with objects. Perhaps it was Robbe-Grillet's anesthetic style—the frigidity of his writing, the sense of keeping it all in—that attracted her. More likely her own interest in philosophy, her urgency to get at ideas that might explain human complexities beyond the scenes and characters of literature, led her to Robbe-Grillet, Michel Butor, Marguerite Duras, and the other writers of the *nouveau roman*. Buried in books and ideas, Angela had little sense of identity with things around her, and was growing increasingly remote from her parents and their way of life. Her experiences drove her into a different world. She had become as much an alien in Alabama as she was in Paris; perhaps more. Something was brewing inside her, and once in a while—perhaps when she got a little too tired or a little too drunk—the lid burst off and her emotions spilled over. It was very, very rare. Friends were aware of complex feelings that Angela could not, or would not, articulate. Beneath the dignified exterior, one of them suggests, there was something raging, something almost self-destructive. In practical terms she was disorganized. She left cigarettes burning, she forgot to eat, she rarely remembered to follow the schedules she made. She walked until her feet hurt, she didn't bother about her health much, and friends found themselves coaxing her to do this or that for her own good. She wanted to do everything very well; when she failed because of an inability to organize her life, it occasionally paralyzed her and she could do nothing at all.

"Everything that is happening to Angela today seems out of phase with what I knew about her then. We never spoke of politics at all and we saw each other every day or every other day," Howard Block states. And Angela agrees she had withdrawn altogether from politics. When John Kennedy was shot in November of 1963, it was the absurdity of it all—the whole mess tumbling down around us—that struck her. "This will make things much harder for us now," she commented. "Before, we really thought something could be done for us. Now it won't." Martin Luther King was awarded the Nobel Peace Prize. Angela was struck by the irony of the gesture and said to Howard, "Well, if they want to do that, let them do it." She reacted differently to the news of four little girls blown apart in a Birmingham church. Told of their shattered bodies found in the debris, she felt intense pain. Very quietly she said to her friends in Paris, "Those little girls were friends of my sister."

If she kept much deep inside her that year in Paris, if she worked so hard it seemed obsessive, there were moments when she let go. She had a tremendous affection for the people she really liked. Howard remembers her excitement once when she talked about the Melishes. Her eyes lighted up when she thought of them. She had a kind of sardonic humor and often in the middle of a perfectly serious conversation Howard would see her wink to the side and grin.

One evening after dinner that winter it snowed in Paris. Reverting promptly to childhood, Angela and her roommates rushed outside. Giddily they traveled to every café in sight, drinking a glass of wine at each, and between drinks ran around in the snow—a rare sight in Paris—and wrote mildly obscene messages in the soft white powder on the cars. But the excitement of the snowy night was mild compared to Angela's enthusiasm over a North Vietnamese Têt celebration.

In Helsinki two years earlier the Cubans had had a great impact on Angela. Their commitment and energy immensely attracted her, but what struck her most was their togetherness, the solidarity they had shown, the hundreds of people linking arms and dancing into the streets. The Têt celebrations in Paris outshone even Helsinki. With a Vietnamese friend, a girl from Saigon who favored the NLF (and was eventually deported from America while studying there), Angela journeyed to a vast sports arena just outside the city. It was already filling up with people who had brought lunch and planned to stay late on into the night. There were anti-American satires, funny skits, much singing. Swaying and singing with the crowds, Angela felt again the excitement she had known slightly during the Easter peace marches in New York and at Helsinki. Her first contacts with people from Third World countries—Cuba, Algeria, Vietnam—were joyous ones. She opened up, if only for an hour or a day. She had a taste of people working together for something that mattered. She liked the feeling.

The year came to an end. Angela's French was fluent; she had completed her courses. According to a close friend, Manfred Clemenz urged her to stay on, and offered, in his European way, to make their engagement formal. He stated that he had no money and that marriage must wait a year or two, until he received his doctorate. In fact, Angela says that there was no engagement, and certainly none was announced publicly. She decided to return to the United States to resume her studies at Brandeis.

Paris had made its contribution and it was time to leave. She had spent much of her year overworking—the rest went to sitting in cafés, talking endlessly, considering the absurdity of the human race. It was a passive year but Angela knew she was simply biding her time. It was a lesson she taught Madame Lamotte's young daughter, a child Angela was very fond of and who loved her in return. As the smallest in a big family, the girl always got the worst teasing and was always last in line; hand-me-downs were her way of life. Frequently she dissolved into tears. Angela sat down one day with the child, according to Madame Lamotte, and explained something important to her. There is no way, she said, that you can get back at them now; you must wait until you've accomplished something, until you've achieved a measure of power and rights of your own. Only then can you get back at those who oppress you and treat you badly. You've got to bide your time. Angela has no recollection of the incident. Certainly she does not remember counseling patience. Whatever was said, there was an immediate, simple point of contact between the American girl and the French child.

PART IV/A RADICAL PROCESS

8/SENIOR YEAR: A MEETING WITH MARCUSE

". . . There is an answer to the question which troubles the minds of so many men of good will: What are the people in a free society going to do? The answer which I believe strikes at the heart of the matter was given by a young black girl. She said: 'For the first time in our life we shall be free to think about what we are going to do.' "

—HERBERT MARCUSE

Herbert Marcuse did not play Pygmalion to Angela, nor did he effect some magical hocus-pocus that transformed her from an apolitical student of French literature into a radical philosopher. Neither did Angela, at the end of her senior year, spring forth, fully committed and ready for action, from the forehead of Herbert Marcuse. There was no blinding flash of light, no moment of revelation.

What first attracted Angela to Marcuse's philosophy was its criticism of society, the society of here and now. Like a good Marxist, he believes that the purpose of philosophy is not some arcane indulgence in logical or philological acrostics, but is to change the world. Its central purpose is to criticize what exists. "That's what attracted me to philosophy. That and the fact that he's a Marxist," Angela notes. Drawn increasingly toward an involvement with ideas during her year in Paris, she came home looking for a use for them. Marcuse was there to suggest one.

Angela had come home from Paris to finish her last year at Brandeis. She continued her studies in French; success in her field was still a goal, but she had so nearly achieved it that she now began to explore the philosophic concepts that had been competing for time in her mind. Marcuse had been on leave of absence during Angela's first year in college, but although she had never heard him speak, she had already begun to read his books and had developed a serious interest in him as a thinker. She heard him lecture for the first time in the autumn of 1964. Gradually a conviction that she wanted to study philosophy took shape, and this growing preoccupation showed clearly in her senior honors thesis on Alain Robbe-Grillet.

Angela began her thesis while she was living as a counselor in the "French house," where students wishing to talk French all the time could live. She had a chance to practice talking French, something she has never lost the taste for, but she was still pretty much a loner that year, deeply absorbed in her work. She heard Robbe-Grillet speak in 1964 at Boston University, and now used her thesis on him to get into the philosophical problems he raises. She discusses Robbe-Grillet's emergence in the mid-1950s along with the other writers of the *nouveau roman*, and accepts their vision of the breakdown of the old moral order. In a world fragmented and dispersed, the traditional novel, she claims, could no longer reproduce reality. And like these writers', her own sense of the need to change or even eliminate a crumbling order is drawn from her own seemingly fragmented and meaningless world. In her world, as in Robbe-Grillet's, the difficulty of identifying with anything was enormous. "The traditional novel prevents man from perceiving his situation and thereby obstructs the exploration and construction of the future . . . it is precisely this contaminated (the great distance between man and nature) relationship of man and the world which one finds in many of the novels written in France immediately before and after the Second World War. Perception, in the way Robbe-Grillet uses it, is necessary for confronting the world in terms of rational choice." Rational choice and the idea that man could live by it haunted Angela. Later, when in Frankfurt she began to study Kant seriously, these preoccupations became almost an obsession.

Angela's thesis is a succinct and careful piece of academic work that reaches a high intellectual standard. But the brilliance people later saw in her, the spark of imagination, the fire are missing. It is impersonal and remote, the work of a conscientious scholar. Occasionally it rises to something more. It is difficult not to light hungrily on the word "revolutionary" when it shows up in Angela's thesis, though in general she applies it strictly to changes in style. Her writing is colorless for the most part, but in appraising Robbe-Grillet's philosophic ideas (and those of Sartre and Merleau-Ponty on which he draws), it catches fire. The work grows vivid, the writing exciting. The need for man to be less distanced from objects around him, the need for new means, new modes through which to perceive the world impress her. Just as she is interested in the ideas rather than the stories, Angela prefers to deal, not with Robbe-Grillet the man, but with Robbe-Grillet the thinker.

She appears totally uninterested in Robbe-Grillet's life and personality, choosing rather to concentrate on how his concepts are conveyed in his imaginative literature. She is remote and theoretical when describing the writer, her approach is cool and dispassionate. Six years later when she met Jean Genet at UCLA, Angela was to show me that a writer's moral involvement was still what interested her most about him. When Genet lectured one afternoon, numbers of students, anticipating wisdom on French drama, stomped angrily out of the hall where he was discussing his travels with the Black Panthers. He called the students "goldfish in the fishbowl of the university." Angela turned to me in great excitement: "He has this fantastic career, he's very well known as a playwright, and all kinds of people really respect him. And he just says that writing plays is a real luxury in a society that's falling apart. So he's giving up the whole thing. He's traveling around the country, then going back to France to try to get other people involved in what's going on here." Clearly Genet had become a model of involvement.

As Angela completed her thesis and her requirements for graduation she also began a course of studies with Marcuse. Philosophic theory was the focus for her, but with Marcuse she began to see its practical applications. Literature, even highly philosophic literature, began to seem limited when compared with the new channels Marcuse opened up. His effect on her was profound; his brand of Marxism made sense to her, not only in economic and political terms, but in human ones. For as Paul Robinson, author of *The Freudian Left*, writes, "Marcuse has become one of the chief ideologues of the New Left, leading the assault on repressive affluence at home and neo-colonial wars abroad. He has assumed this political role quite readily. He now identifies student antiwar demonstrators, civil rights workers, the oppressed victims of colonialism in Africa and Asia (Fanon's Wretched of the Earth), even hippies as the true descendants of the classical Marxian proletariat."

Born in Berlin in 1898, Herbert Marcuse left Germany on Hitler's rise to power and came to teach in American universities—first Columbia and then, from 1954 to 1967, Brandeis, before moving to the University of California at San Diego, where he is now. Very early he diverged from the German academic tradition in which, as a philosopher, he had grown up, to attack his old teacher Heidegger for irrationalism (Heidegger had become a member of the Nazi Party) and to embrace Marxist materialism. From his earliest writings he was concerned with making philosophy useful to human beings.

In Marcuse's view happiness is the important goal, and

happiness, which he sees as "the fulfillment of all potentialities of the individual," depends on freedom. But even though prosperity in advanced societies has insured freedom from material want, man is still not free. For this Marcuse blames, among other forces, the liberal capitalist order of things, even in its welfare state version, which has imposed new forms of domination in place of the old domination by economic necessity. It has "welded blessing and curse into one rational whole." To absorb the vast productivity made possible by modern technology, people are persuaded to need things—and then to work to satisfy those needs. Work for the voracious machine becomes a value in its own right, and in the process men are distorted from their true natures; even their sexual instincts are distorted.

It was perhaps by putting sex into Marxism that Marcuse really made his name among the young—many of them without the philosophical training to follow the complexities of his thought. His innovation, presented in *Eros and Civilization*, was to apply Freud's insights, particularly his concept of repression, to the operation of control in society. In a later book, *One-Dimensional Man*, Marcuse—who is not very hopeful about the coming of a better society—shows how sexual needs can be artificially created and artificially satisfied, so that even in an apparent permissive age men cannot enjoy their own bodies in a pure, spontaneous, and fully human way. To the "repression in affluence" of advanced societies he opposes a vision of a better world in which man would have "the good conscience to make life an end in itself, to live in joy without fear."

One-Dimensional Man consecrated Marcuse as a guru of the New Left, a new Rousseau, offering to their enchanted imaginations a new nonviolent, nonwasteful, nonexploiting age of innocence. Marcuse has returned the compliment paid him by the students by finding them, along with American blacks and Third World revolutionaries, among the few forces still capable of changing the world. In fact he has often gone out on a more practical limb by supporting the young in their demonstrations and protests against established society.

Carl Oglesby, in *The New Left Reader*, suggests that Marcuse has produced few activists, but "has informed many. He is someone to be read after the membrane of silence or noncommitment has been ruptured and he is a major source of the New Left's conceptualization of its world and its tasks." It was doubtless on this level that he influenced Angela.

When she first read his books, and later attended his lectures at Brandeis, it was a purely intellectual excitement she felt—the enthusiastic recognition that elements of her own experience were here being fitted into a rigorous intellectual interpretation of our age. She had seen for herself the drawbacks of affluence, she had felt in her own pulses the hopeful promise represented by the activists of the Third World. And now Marcuse was making sense of what she had seen and felt. She told me, "I never cease to stand in awe of his ability to relate ideas, ostensibly buried under the sands of time, to the current situation we have to deal with in our social and political lives." Although not yet ready to turn activist herself, she began to share Marcuse's prophetic vision of a better life for human beings which would allow them to fulfill themselves, to be more creative, to become other than automatons in a mechanical society, to move from one-dimensional creatures to flesh-and-blood men with minds, passions, ideas.

June came and Angela was graduated with high honors. College was over, Marcuse's influence remained. He encouraged her to apply for a scholarship to study at the Institute for Social Research at the Goethe University in Frankfurt.

Marcuse explains, "I sent her to my friend Adorno at Frankfurt to learn the philosophy I taught at Brandeis, the philosophy I had studied myself. Adorno was deeply impressed by her." The Institute, when Marcuse was there in the early 1930s, had on the faculty Max Horkheimer, Frederick Pollock, Erich Fromm, Theodor Adorno. It was the most important and prestigious center in the world for the study of German Idealism and, of course, Marxism.

Marcuse was to find a great change in Angela when he met her again. "Already in San Diego I noticed a definite change. But at Brandeis she was not yet at all active in black politics. There was a strange incubation period, a period during which Angela showed little of the political being which later appeared. I think the big question is what brought about the change."

9 / GERMANY: PHILOSOPHY AND POLITICS

"Act only on that maxim whereby thou canst at the same time
will that it should become a universal law."

—IMMANUEL KANT

Frankfurt is not a city that reaches out with warmth
and charm to greet arriving strangers. It is a cold, stark city
of eight hundred thousand inhabitants that was bombed flat
in the war and rose again from the shambles an organized
well-planned town with skyscrapers, office buildings, hotels,
porno palaces, exhibition halls, and carparks. It was as un-
welcoming as it was efficient when Angela arrived there in
the summer of 1965 with only Marcuse's encouragement,
a new B.A. degree, and the promise of a German government grant to study at the university. She barely spoke German; her lingering attachment to Manfred Clemenz dis-
integrated quickly after meeting him again. She had no
more idea of what to expect from the future than of where
to find a room.

She walked through Frankfurt looking for lodgings and
was rewarded with a small but sharp taste of German racism. Checking a list from the student housing bureau, she
shyly called on landladies who when they saw her promptly
said, "Full up." Some, peering suspiciously through the
crack of a door, refused to talk to her at all. The population
of Frankfurt was as white as its new buildings. People turned
often to look at Angela in the street, some of them taking
her for the daughter of a black GI. The stares made her

squirm and walk faster; she felt the discomfort of a creature in a glass bowl even when passersby looked at her from simple curiosity or with admiration rather than prejudice. In the end her housing problem was ingeniously solved.

An ancient disused factory in the Adalbertstrasse, near Frankfurt's university, was scheduled for demolition when David Wittenberg, a stocky genial student, took over the building and rented bits of it to friends and colleagues for next to nothing. Most of the inhabitants of the "Factory" were university students and many were in the SDS (Sozialistischer Deutscher Studentenbund—German Socialist Students' League). Angela was then going out with a young German named Tommy Mitscherlich who lived at the Factory, and she moved into a room upstairs.

Elfie Hieber, a small, fair-haired, mild-mannered young woman, was a sociology student at the university and also a resident at the Factory, which she describes as a vast, cheerless shell of a building where the heating never worked through the long frozen German winters. The ground floor had two big communal rooms. The warren of offices on the next two floors was converted into rooms that the new and very lively tenants filled with posters, books, wine bottles, and all the paraphernalia of student life. The "hole" was a cavernous cellar in the building's bowels where anyone could do anything—especially when the need to let off steam became too pressing. One of Angela's neighbors was a young man named Hans Jurgen Krahl, a leader of the SDS and one of the most brilliant, neurotic, and emphatic people in Frankfurt. Krahl drank a great deal of potent German spirits and beer and, coming home to the Factory at night, he often descended to the hole to hurl bottles, one after the other, against the wall. Hearing the shattering glass—and having witnessed Krahl's play-acting at suicide—Angela would huddle in her room, terrified by the man's violence. Later, though, she became friends with Krahl and drew on his brilliance and knowledge in long discussions of Kant.

Other fears surrounded Angela when she first went to the Factory. Elfie Hieber remembers that she hardly spoke to anyone, a fact that Elfie, who considered Americans the most open of people, outgoing and talkative from the first meeting, at first attributed to the language problem. The way of life in the Factory helped after a while. The constant flow of people and ideas, the lack of structure, the absence of restrictions, were liberating after a life spent obeying rules. Until then Angela had docilely observed her family's protective restraints, the rules of other families she had lived with, the conventions and requirements of school and college. Now she was on her own, but lonely, and it took her some months to feel really at home. There was great excitement powering the first attempts at communal life among German students.

The heyday of the German student movement and its idea of communal life had barely begun when Angela arrived in Frankfurt, and the Factory was but a preview of what was to come in the boomtime of 1967. Communal living (as well as day-care centers and everything that goes with it) was an experiment in integrating life within which the political, the intellectual, and the personal merged, overcoming the inevitable contradictions faced by middle-class students intent on revolution. Erich Fried, a German poet and radical, explains that the students were trying to create an environment, a milieu, a way of life that reflected their essentially anti-authoritarian radical politics. Life in the communes was a twenty-four-hour discussion group. If there was a structure at all, it was invisible, for the movement, intellectually and politically, hung its hat firmly on the peg marked anti-authoritarian. Everyone somehow managed to do as he pleased and also to work with the others. More or less everyone ate together, worked together, played together, and slept together. Most of all they talked. It was very easy-going and relaxed; what held it together were the fine, steely, exciting tensions of change.

Angela began to loosen up a little. She learned some German, began her studies, and just occasionally took down the polite screen when she talked to her neighbors. Eventually her friendship with Tommy Mitscherlich cooled off. Often she stayed alone in her bleak room, working or simply sitting, but in time she talked to Elfie, who, though enormously interested in Angela's childhood, was reluctant to pry. Shy and reserved, Angela was very pleased, almost eager when people came to see her, but she never made the first move. When she talked with Elfie about Alabama, she was careful not to recite the old stories everyone already knew, but spoke about the bombings she had seen herself, and about her father's warning not to go into certain playgrounds. As at Brandeis, she was still refusing to dine out on the "Southern horror story." Slowly, as her trust and her grasp of German increased, Angela opened up.

Her capacity for self-discipline remained striking—although there were dramatic lapses. She soon acquired a very reasonable ability to read in German by comparing texts, working out sentence structure and looking up every unfamiliar word in the dictionary. Elfie notes that one seminar was so difficult that she herself quit while Angela completed the course. There were days when she worked compulsively for ten or twelve hours.

But there were also days when she sat huddled on her bed in the cold room doing nothing at all. This periodic inability to work, of which there had been hints at college, now showed itself more seriously. It amounted almost to a disease whose symptoms were a striking incapacity to deal with practical matters. An Italian journalist, Claudio Pozzvoli, who saw her often in Frankfurt, says she found it exceedingly difficult to arrange the simple everyday details of life: clothes didn't get to the cleaner, there was nothing to eat when dinnertime came. It distressed her that she should be unable to take care of her own business. She was intensely anxious much of the time. Her movements were awkward and unharmonious, her gestures jerky and unsure like those of someone who has lost his way in a city and stands paralyzed, uncertain where to turn, wishing someone would come along with directions and take over. One afternoon, Elfie recalls, in an effort to find something in her room, Angela rushed about in circles and suddenly knocked over a whole bookcase made of flimsy upended orange crates. The books spilled out across the room, creating a shambles. Should she clean up the room and be late for an appointment? Should she simply close the door on the mess and face cleaning it later? Decision was impossible. Intellectually she ran on reason—or wanted to. There must be a manner in which the wheels turned and chores got done in a rational, orderly way, she knew there must.

Coexisting with Angela's lack of practical sense was her obsession with work. The two went together, faces of the same coin. On days when she did nothing her disgust with herself paralyzed her further. Her problems were deeply rooted in conflicts that were both personal and social. At the simplest level, she felt she had to do better than everyone else and accomplish more. Having been singled out from most other blacks, privilege became her burden. How many others could send their children to college, to study in Paris and in Germany? The sense of specialness she had felt all her life was exaggerated, coated with a thin layer of guilt, and this was aggravated by her feeling that she was "always just leaving" as things happened. (She'd left the South for Elisabeth Irwin as the Freedom Rides began; she arrived in Frankfurt the summer Watts burned.)

Angela's problems with work and the awkward way she dealt with everyday living went together with her complicated attitude toward being an outsider and toward rebellion, as well as to her search for identity. Gradually she was able to clear the path toward self-definition of some of the guilt, obsessiveness, and alienation that obscured it. She began the weeding out when she underwent a period of psychoanalytic therapy.

Tommy Mitscherlich, the young man who had brought her into the Factory, is the son of one of the foremost psychoanalysts in Germany. Professor Alexander Mitscherlich is not only a prominent analyst, he is also widely honored for his work as an experimental scientist and as a social psychologist; he is an internationally respected figure. Before Tommy Mitscherlich's friendship with Angela ended and he went on to Berlin to study at the film institute, he took her home to Heidelberg to meet his father. After seeing Angela, Professor Mitscherlich arranged for her to begin therapy in Frankfurt. She continued in therapy until she left Germany, almost two years later.

Elfie recalls that Angela actively disliked the process; the simple act of arriving at a given place at a given time was difficult enough, and the continual baring of herself to another, a painful process for anyone, was doubly so for a person so reticent and withdrawn. At the end of two years of analysis she would admit to Elfie that it had done her a great deal of good, that however painful the process had been, it was necessary. If Angela saw a great improvement in herself over the two years, her friends were for their part sure she fitted her skin better. Not only had she fewer problems getting down to work; not only was she more open with people, less defensive, less guarded; but even her gestures were more graceful, she rarely dropped things, she seemed altogether more in control of her life.

During those years life became more interesting in Frankfurt. Angela began to make friends, for if she failed to reach out, people were always attracted toward her. She was a complete intellectual, friends say. She liked parties and dancing but she didn't need them; she enjoyed political meetings, her classes, and whatever rallies or demonstrations were on at the moment; but what she loved most were endless drawn-out discussions with someone else, on a one-to-one basis. She drew on different friends for their ideas—on Claudio's knowledge of practical politics, on Krahl's philosophic acumen. Imaginative literature still held her interest, but more and more it was the writer's commitment that was important. To be in the world seemed a very important goal.

Being in the world had, for Angela, been a complex and frequently frustrating experience. She had always been an outsider. Self-protection called for a series of masks to put on, a variety of screens through which to show only selected images of herself. It mattered little whether the image was that of the good daughter at home, the cultivated student at Brandeis, the preoccupied intellectual in Paris. Whatever the image, underneath it she was constantly searching for an identity and a solidarity with others to give relief from her sense of specialness. At last in Frankfurt, although she was still an outsider, she began to feel comfortable.

Hundreds of foreigners turned up every year at Frankfurt University, every one of them an outsider, and to be alienated among the alienated is really to belong. All were rebelling, all clung together for support. Angela was not singled out either for racial attacks or for special attention. As in those moments she had spent with the Algerians and Vietnamese in Paris, and with the Cubans in Helsinki, she found among the Frankfurt students a world with potential for her. Almost everyone she knew in Frankfurt was intellectual, many were fine theoreticians, and many more were involved in psychoanalysis. While most of her friends in Frankfurt were young white Germans, she felt the need for links with home and with black people. She met and grew friendly with a black ex-GI who had stayed on in Germany after finishing his army service. Together they discussed news of the movement from home, and tried to "build a kind of bridge between Germany and black experience." It was an important friendship, one Angela recalls as essential for her at that time.

As she probed more and more deeply into herself, into philosophy and into politics, she came to believe that a synthesis of all those things was necessary.

Philosophy and politics were both taken seriously in the Germany Angela knew, but when she first arrived in 1965, there was not much political activity. Politics were, on the whole, still strictly theoretical, a fact that Angela accepted with equanimity: theory, on which she at first seemed shaky to the philosophically accomplished German students, still represented for her the supreme value of Left-wing existence. She had a chance both to investigate this notion and to brush up her theoretical techniques at the lectures given at the Goethe University's Institute for Social Research by Marcuse's friend Theodor Adorno, who has been described by Erich Fried as "the man who trained an entire generation of students in critical thinking."

After some courses in literature and a lot of hard work on her own, Angela mastered enough German to turn her studies to Kant, Hegel, and Marx. Marcuse had encouraged her to go to Frankfurt in the belief that properly to study Marx and his predecessors, Kant and Hegel, it was necessary to work in German: the English translations were not adequate, the vocabulary simply did not exist in foreign languages. But a mere reading knowledge of German was not enough. Adorno's classes were considered the most difficult at the Institute—even German students had trouble with his language. When the time came for Angela to write her major seminar paper for Adorno, she had to call on German friends to help with the wording, but the ideas were her own.

The course of studies at the Institute was a traditional combination of the social sciences and philosophy, with a strong emphasis on German Idealism; everyone studied the philosophy of the Enlightenment and there were seminars in the history of philosophy and in philosophical history— two separate branches of intellectual activity. For Angela work at the Institute was not just a scanning of the intellectual horizons for personal or social salvation. Nor was she driven only by the compulsion to succeed. She deeply enjoyed philosophy: the discipline excited her mind profoundly.

Professor Oskar Negt, one of the leading teachers at the Frankfurt Institute, believes "She was acquiring the knowledge that dialectical thinking consists mainly in becoming more sensitive to social experience . . . that the decisive insights of her Frankfurt studies, the studies of philosophy, helped her see the ways to effect social change." In 1966, halfway through her time in Germany, Negt counseled Angela to concentrate her studies on Kant. She took up the suggestion eagerly. In a *Der Stern* article, Negt quotes her:

> As all concepts, the concept of interest raised by Kant has a double meaning. The philosopher describes the moral (reason) interest through which people create their moral laws and which is beautifully described in the "categorical imperative: to act always so that the law of your wanting can be the general law for humans." When all people would behave accordingly, the highest level of human freedom would be achieved. A

class society would not exist nor would racial discrimination. But from the same breast where the moral
interest comes, comes the "physical interest": considering everything for one's own advantage. Kant, the philosopher of the bourgeoisie, had an uncorruptible insight into the incompatibility of these two interest
levels.

"Angela was fascinated by the pathos of the realization," Negt adds. "The consequence was that only on a
higher level—the Marxist-Socialist level—would it be possible to unite these contradictions."

By mid-1966 the German student body was beginning
to move into active political involvement. For Angela there
was no great moment of truth, no moment in which she saw
her path to political commitment illumined by streaks of
philosophical lightning. But while new ideas were taking
shape through her intellectual pursuits in Germany, she was
also learning much from the activities of the SDS. She was
not a leader, nor to her German friends did she give any
sign of becoming one. She was shy and wanted to be unob-
vious, a small hard-working part of the radical political
endeavor. Even her appearance conformed to the unobtru-
sive pattern. While she wore her hair in an Afro, she dressed
simply and unremarkably.

The upsurge of radical German student movement
coincided with Angela's last year in Frankfurt, when the
changes that had been incubating slowly started to grow
more rapidly as America escalated its involvement in the
Vietnam War. Antiwar feeling, the anti-authoritarian movement that began in the university, and the political situation
in Germany itself combined to push the students out of
their theorizing and into the streets. Frankfurt, a traditional center for Marxist studies, was in the vanguard.

The Vietnam War was not simply a useful pretext for leftist student groups to latch on to as a cover for their activities. At its core it was for many young people a profound symbol of Western authoritarianism and hypocrisy, against which the German (and other) radical students reacted with personal revulsion: for, as Rudi Dutschke put it, "Today we are not bound together by an abstract theory of history but an existential disgust in the presence of a society which chatters about liberty and yet brutally oppresses the immediate interests and needs of individuals and peoples fighting for their social and economic emancipation." The Vietnam War, with other Third World struggles, was crucial to the student rebellion in Germany and elsewhere. Unpermissive Soviet Russia no longer attracted the young. New idols came from the hills of the underdeveloped countries. The colonial revolutions in Algeria, Cuba, China, and Vietnam fathered concepts and heroes who, as Marcuse had noted, deeply touched the imagination of the young as nothing in their own societies could have done.

But if Vietnam was a cause in its own right, it was also an example to be applied elsewhere. Politicized by the napalm and the B-52s, the student rebellion developed, in Dutschke's phrase, "with real virulence only . . . in the antiauthoritarian struggle against the bureaucracy within the milieu of the university." The German University, David Wittenberg remarks, was an anachronism. It kept you happy like a child, dependent, yet free to make of it what you would and could. You emerged eventually, prepared for absolutely nothing. The pattern was kept rigidly in place by the professors who were little kings, by the "dictatorship of examinations," and ultimately by the state. Seen as a microcosm of authoritarian society at large, the university gradually became for the radicals a symbol of the state, and as such ripe for overthrow.

Even before the movement against war abroad and authority at home had got off the ground, the German Social Democrats had done their bit to radicalize the young. In a country where "socialism" meant the other Germany over the Wall, where the Communist Party was banned (from 1956 to 1969), where Social Democrat could cooperate with Christian Democrat to form a government, any sign of Left-wing militancy among the young was liable to panic their elders into overreaction. This happened in 1960 when the youth division of the Social Democrats was expelled for its undilutedly socialist program, and once outside the restraining influence of the party, the young had nowhere to go but further to the left—which, over the years, they enthusiastically did.

With anti-authoritarianism so high on its list of priorities, the SDS resisted becoming a closely structured organization. Personal and social emancipation, as taught by Marcuse and Adorno, was an essential target, and the SDS concerned itself with the personal experience of the individual as much as it did with the economic working of society. It even generated some forerunners of "encounter groups." People listened to one another, Erich Fried notes, and if there was a kind of elitism, it was very goodhearted: ultraintellectual students would assume that young workers were as capable as themselves of taking in the extraordinarily complex tomes considered essential to political education. Under the large loose blanket of the SDS a variety of factions—Maoist, Trotskyite, revisionist—coexisted peaceably, giving rise from time to time to short-lived and extravagantly titled organizations, such as the Viva Maria, named after Louis Malle's film in which Jeanne Moreau was held to symbolize Leninist strategy while Brigitte Bardot was the realization of anarchism: the goal, of course, was a synthesis of the two. Activity within the SDS included writing, organizing demonstrations, and endless dialogue. They talked, turning over ideas, clarifying, defining, inventing, theorizing, planning. Angela took part in all this, enjoying the solidarity, the intellectual exercises—and the lighter moments. "We also talked a lot of the time about blah-blah, in other words gossip," recalls David Wittenberg.

By 1967 the movement had changed and grown, and Angela with it. No longer did she blunder helplessly about; much surer of herself and her direction, she had achieved poise. Returning to Frankfurt from San Diego, where he had been studying with Marcuse, Lothar Menne, a charming, mercurial young man who knew her well, found few of the awkward characteristics that had been so noticeable two years earlier. The two became good friends. Angela had become an interesting, hardworking, determined young woman, attractive and intelligent, often wry, occasionally sarcastic, with whom he could swap notes on the music of Pete Seeger and on other movement songs ("Down in the Dungeon," "The Halls are Made of Marble," "This Land Is Your Land," "If I Had a Hammer") and on the Communist Party. In her Frankfurt years, Lothar remembers, Angela displayed for the Communist Party a half-mocking, half-nostalgic attachment, simultaneously sentimental and satirical.

Meanwhile she was working harder with the SDS. In fact everyone was working harder, for in 1967 the vast anti-student campaign began in Germany. Carl Oglesby writes:

> The new activists acquire their radical antiauthoritarianism at the end of police sticks that are swinging from one end of the earth to the other in behalf of everything dead and dry, in defense of social orders that prosper by denying life its possibilities and that greet every new aspiration with increasing indifference, deri-

sion and violence. The policeman's riot club functions like a magic wand under whose hard caress the banal soul grows vivid and the nameless recover their authenticity—a bestower, this want, of the lost charisma of the modern self: I bleed, therefore I am. This is a ferocious but effective way to be a student—to be educated.

Adorno has drawn an analogy between the role the students played in 1967–68 and the role of the Jews under Nazism. Taking his point, some students appeared wearing the yellow armbands that the Jews were forced to wear by Hitler. The reactionary West German newspaper magnate, Axel Springer, fostered the attitude that students were parasites and vermin whom the old regime would have known how to deal with; and many of Springer's vast reading audience shared his views. Demonstrations against the war were often met by brutal police attacks; the man-in-the-street was all too happy to spit on a passing student; another, lying bleeding in the street, might feel the heavy boot of a cab driver in his ribs. Then Beno Ohnesorg, an onlooker at a Berlin demonstration, was killed. He was beaten up and fell to the ground, calling to the police, "For God's sake, don't shoot!" An officer shot him. For Angela, as for the other students, the murderous repression of the ruling classes defending their position was demonstrated beyond all doubt. But she was not tempted to believe that this was a problem confined to Germany.

By the spring of 1967 Angela was growing more and more anxious to get home, according to Claudio Pozzvoli. Her paper for Adorno was finished and in any case the choice of staying or going wasn't wholly her own: her grant was running out. Before she left, though, she accomplished one final task. There was to be a Congress on the Dialectics of

Liberation in London that summer, and as Lothar Menne recalls, endless pow-wows were held on how to raise the money to get to London to attend it. An old out-of-print text by Professor Horkheimer was dredged up; if five hundred copies were typed, mimeographed, and sold, they would bring in the price of the tickets to England. Most who embarked on this ambitious project gave up from exhaustion or boredom. Angela sat up and typed through the night.

With Germany behind her and California ahead, this detour to London provided Angela with a decisive experience: she met Stokely Carmichael.

Born in the West Indies, Carmichael had been active on the radical wing of the American civil rights movement, but just a year earlier had stopped working with whites to become the best-known and most aggressively militant spokesman for Black Power. Scornful of the implicit acceptance he found among blacks in the United States that to be black was somehow shameful, that it should be ignored as far as possible and social justice fought for on the grounds that this was the right of all citizens, Carmichael had founded the Black Panthers in Lowndes County, Alabama. Formed originally to work for rural reform, the Black Panther Party was, by 1967, preaching black separatism—and black self-defense: Carmichael was the first to demand that blacks arm themselves.

After years of assuming that justice should be striven for in a context of nonviolent integration, Angela found Stokely's new gospel a revelation. Not that she accepted it on his mere say-so, but that such startling things should be stirring among American blacks was intensely exciting. For the moment she filed away the lessons she was learning in order to concentrate on the London conference, but as soon as she got home she meant to learn more about these developments. Another plank in Stokely Carmichael's program was solidarity with Black Africa: while American blacks supported the Black Africans' struggles for freedom from oppression and neocolonialism, the Black African countries should use what economic power they had to pressure the United States into granting justice to its citizens. In line with his pan-blackism, Carmichael married the South African folk singer Miriam Makeba and eventually went to live in Africa, in Sekou Touré's Guinea, where he still is.

In London Angela, Lothar Menne and other friends stayed with the English radical Robin Blackburn, in the immigrant slum Notting Hill, visiting black neighborhoods between lectures at an experimental theater, the Roundhouse, by Marcuse, Carmichael, and R. D. Laing (the existential psychiatrist, who in *The Politics of Experience* argues that it is society, not the schizophrenics whom society rejects, that is sick). With Carmichael and the English black power leader Michael X, Angela had her first taste of organizing, and it helped to make the future clearer. She identified with the people she met, finding that, as Kenneth Keniston puts it, "identification with others who are oppressed is more important and more motivating than one's own deprivation." A plan was evolving by way of reason that led from a disordered life to one that made sense. She saw the task of the intellectual and of the organizer in the streets as basically the same: to make changes; to make revolution. At that moment Angela could have started down the straight and narrow to simple academic excellence either in Germany or America. She knew herself too well now. It was time to get out of the ivory tower.

"If we're going to have a bloodbath, let's get it over with."

—RONALD REAGAN

"I noticed a big change when she came to San Diego. It was in the form of a change to action. In America again, seeing the way black people live and being in touch with the black community—especially after Germany—this led to what she had to become," Marcuse says.

The excitement and enthusiasm sparked by her meeting with Stokely Carmichael and the visits to London's ghetto sent Angela home burning to see what had emerged in the black movement in America. She stopped off in Birmingham, where, Mrs. Davis remembers, the first thing she asked for was her favorite dish: collard greens and cornbread. After a short visit, she grew restless, feeling the distance between herself and her family greater than ever. She argued about politics with her father, and after visiting a few friends, she quickly packed for the trip to California. Before she left Alabama, however, she went along to rap with the Muslim minister in Birmingham; she just had to learn more about this development of a separate black consciousness, so opposed to the old slogan "black and white unite." What price the old high school song now—"The ink is black, the paper's white, together we learn to read and write. . . ."?

Why did she choose California? Largely because Marcuse was there, in San Diego, and she wanted to begin work on her doctorate with him. She could have gone elsewhere —her work at Brandeis and in Germany had been outstanding—but she no longer wanted to look down on the scene below from an intellectual perch in some Ivy League or Eastern university. Her participation in student politics in Frankfurt had given her a taste for direct involvement, and in the San Diego–Los Angeles region there was a large and active black community.

The changes she saw in black people amazed Angela but more than anything they delighted her. What she felt was gut-level, deep. There was a "beautiful solidarity implied in the way we were sisters and brothers to one another. I can remember the time when you could walk down a street in LA and know that if a brother or sister with a natural passed you by, there would be a spontaneous reaching out in the words, 'What's going on, sister?' "

California supplied Marcuse and it supplied blacks; but in any case in the Davis family mythology it was a good place for a new start. Fania Davis says, "I always wanted to come out here. Even years ago I thought of it as a big wide-open place." Having finished Swarthmore, where she had majored in French, Fania followed her sister's footsteps to study philosophy on the West Coast. To both sisters, children of the industrial South, the urban East, and European-oriented education, the West offered new horizons, bigger spaces, more possibilities. The last decades have seen every kind of organization, from the John Birch Society to the Black Panther Party, take root and bloom in the fertile California soil. All the contradictions of America travel bumper to bumper down the freeways to extremes. It's beautiful, it's going barefoot in the library, its getting in your car and driving miles without seeing anything but the mountains, or crawling past an endless strip of carwashes that look like Byzantine motels, motels that resemble nothing so much as carparks, and taco stands that talk. It's plastic and it's the future. It's a state that attracts enormous numbers of creative and talented people, where experiments in every field gain acclaim. A state that wins Nobel Prizes. It's the richest state in America, richer than all but a few of the world's nations; everything grows here: grapes and oranges, redwoods and palms, all slightly larger than life. Buildings rise, colleges flourish, migrant workers strike for a living wage, surplus fruit is burned, ghettos explode.

San Diego is a city that pretty well fulfills the American Dream. A very modern backwater, it is Nixonland metaphorically and in reality; traditionally a Navy town, it has become a staging point for shipments of men and supplies to Vietnam. The industry, noise, and fumes of Los Angeles have barely invaded peaceful San Diego. Smog is just a rumor two hours away up the freeway. People are satisfied in San Diego and with it. It is a pretty shining place and everyone there talks incessantly of its charms. The climate is lovely, the Pacific vistas with Mexico a shadow in the near distance are impressive. The air seems to clean out your lungs as you wander through Balboa Park, one of the most attractive green spaces in the country, and the San Diego Zoo is the biggest and best in the world. Most of the people live on a series of suburban hills in bright new houses. It is the good life. There is no center in San Diego, no neighborhoods and no personality. Happily for the largely white population, the Logan Heights ghetto is not too visible.

San Diego contains some of the most entrenched conservatives in the state, perhaps because the very rootlessness of the place they have come to settle in drives them to put down traditions. Like many Californians, the people here have fought for what they've got, having moved West to grab a little piece of space, a little of what's left of America.

And, says Neil Morgan, "in his quest for the full life, the Californian looks to his educational system and in particular to the gargantuan University of California. He feels proprietary about it. He regards its hippies and its radicals as interfering with his fulfillment."

The University of California became an enormously desirable place for young academics in the early 1960s. It was dynamic, it was heavily funded, its faculty was superb, there was plenty of skiing. Against a glorious backdrop of mountain and sea life ran smoothly—until politics became as much a way of life as sport at the university. Events like the Berkeley Free Speech Movement in 1965, the controversy over Marcuse's right to teach in San Diego, the firing of Angela Davis from UCLA in 1969 finally burst the complacent if creative bubble. Much of this change came to pass under the increasingly malignant rule of Ronald Reagan, who as head of the Board of Regents virtually reigns over the university system.

The University of California at San Diego is at La Jolla, fifteen minutes north of the city, just inland from the Pacific Ocean. Angela arrived in the autumn of 1967 on the campus, which spreads in leisurely fashion across the mesa dotted with eucalyptus and rising above the very blue sea. There is an easy, open atmosphere at UCSD. The bright ingenuous California sky shines overhead, students wander about barefoot in bright summer clothes. Fountains play, the sun keeps shining, people smile. The buildings seem to rise naturally from the ground as if redwood and stone and glass had come spontaneously together in elegant designs. With the Salk Institute nearby, the university, which grew out of the Scripps Oceanographic Institution, is part of an intellectual community of some scope. UCSD has three colleges now, the first of twelve planned to be built along the lines of Oxford colleges, each with its own residence hall, dining hall, and provost. "The mood is euphoric at San Diego," someone said.

One of the main intellectual attractions at UCSD is Professor Herbert Marcuse. Under his guidance Angela completed her master's degree in a year, and in the autumn of 1968 passed her qualifying exams to begin work on her dissertation. Her thesis plan was a study called, "Toward a Kantian Theory of Force." She also worked as Marcuse's teaching assistant. Marcuse, looking very much at home in his sunny office with its view of the campus, welcomes students who stop to peer through the open door with a question. His affection for the young is obvious. Over his desk is a mobile that sways in the ocean breeze, the letters L O V E jiggling slightly. Marcuse wrote in his political preface to *Eros and Civilization*:

> Can we speak of a juncture between the erotic and political dimension? In and against the deadly efficient organization of the affluent society, not only radical protest, but even the attempt to formulate, to articulate, to give word to protest assume a childlike, ridiculous immaturity. Thus it is ridiculous and perhaps "logical" that the Free Speech Movement at Berkeley terminated in the row caused by the appearance of a sign with the four-letter word. It is perhaps equally ridiculous and right to see deeper significance in the buttons worn by some of the demonstrators (among them infants) against the slaughter in Vietnam: MAKE LOVE, NOT WAR.

Marcuse speaks of Angela with great affection. She is a total human being, he says, not merely an expression of this idea or that concept. She is shy, not self-contained, not introverted, and not in any way self-centered, but rather the contrary, open to people and enjoying friendship. As soon as a contact is established with her, she talks not only with her whole mind but with her whole soul. Her warmth is unusual and she is in no way a calculating person, never overcautious in her emotions and reactions. Her intellectual honesty is great, her need to discuss problems and work them out imperative. "In semir..rs," he adds, "she talked a great deal. She was a good discusser and she could write and read! She was, though I am tired of repeating it, certainly one of the three most, if not *the* most, intelligent students I have had in thirty years. An ideal student, she had a very high intelligence, she did the work easily. But she was not only brain. She loved to talk. There was joy and great confidence and there was never any despair. She thought and felt with her whole personality." That was later. Angela initially found San Diego a little solitary.

She had arrived from Europe, burning to make her contribution, a need that had grown during her years as an American abroad. James Baldwin has put into words in his essay "The Discovery of What It Means To Be an American" this duty toward his own country that some expatriates learn in Europe.

> . . . One day it begins to be borne in on the writer, and with great force, that he is living in Europe as an American. If he were living there as a European, he would be living on a different and far less attractive continent.
>
> This crucial day may be the day on which an Algerian taxi driver tells him how it feels to be an Algerian in Paris. It may be the day on which he passes a café terrace and catches a glimpse of the tense, intelligent and troubled face of Albert Camus. Or it may be the day on which someone asks him to explain Little Rock and he begins to feel that it would be simpler—

and, corny as the word sounds—more honorable—to *go* to Little Rock than sit in Europe, on an American passport, trying to explain it.

This is a personal day, a terrible day, the day to which his entire sojourn has been tending. It is the day he realizes that there are no untroubled countries in this fearfully troubled world; that if he has been preparing himself for anything in Europe, he has been preparing himself—for America. In short, the freedom that the American writer finds in Europe brings him, full circle, back to himself, with the responsibility for his development where it always was: in his own hands.

In the intervals of her studies, Angela sought an organization in which to do her American duty. It seemed perfectly simple to her: you just asked around. With amusement she now recalls her own naïveté. No one was anxious to trust this bright, eager girl who suddenly appeared in San Diego to rush around and ask how she could help in the struggle, and understandably enough, rumors began to circulate that she was an agent of the security services. Perplexed and disappointed, she took to walking alone on the beach or drove to San Diego to stroll around the Logan Heights ghetto. It was a lonely time: she felt able to identify with her people, more conscious than ever before of the oppression they suffered, but no one seemed to want her or her insights.

Eventually, with some other blacks, she began canvassing the campus to see if a black student union could be formed. Gradually adherents were drawn in. At a leftist meeting one day Angela saw a boy and girl, both light-skinned and with reddish hair like herself, standing at the back. She wasn't sure they were blacks because she wasn't wearing her glasses and couldn't see well at a distance. Both joined the group—and it turned out that they had wondered the same about her. Then an incident occurred which gave the newly formed group a focus. A black man named Eddie Lynn, stationed at the Naval base in San Diego, protested against racism in the Navy and was subjected to harassment. Slowly, using this incident and others, the group began to expand, and to her dismay Angela found herself emerging as a leader. Her old unwillingness to assert herself, an expression of her shyness and insecurity, was translated into an ideological distrust of the personality cult. Attention paid to a person tended to be, she believed, attention diverted from a cause—a reading of the situation that was, with her arrest and trial, to gain ironic point: in the campaign to "Free Angela Davis" the issues Angela Davis was fighting for would drop somewhat out of sight. But to begin with, she was also quite simply diffident about her abilities to lead. "For a while I guess I was considered something of a leader, although I did not really like the role; I assumed it merely because others were unwilling to and pushed me into it." Yet she made an effort to acquire the main tool of a leader who trades in revolution: rhetoric.

At the beginning of her political career in San Diego her audiences understood little of what Angela said when she spoke in public. Her discourse was so "high-flown," so laced with complex philosophical terms, that few listeners made sense of her speeches. Slowly she learned to be a speechmaker. She learned to project herself, learned the bombastic, passionate style of public speaking that a Brandeis friend suggests is merely another screen through which she filters only what she wants seen or heard. Others remark, "It isn't Angela." In private Angela's voice is soft and gentle, her diction impeccable, her language precise, and her style familiar to anyone educated in the Western intellectual tradition. When she spoke in public, however, she was interested in reaching a wide spectrum of people.

Marcuse's explication of revolutionary language makes

sense: "Radical denial of the establishment and the communication of the new consciousness depends more and more fatefully on a language of their own as all communication is monopolized and validated by the one-dimensional society." He explains that the language of the radicals takes sublime concepts from the Western society they want to overthrow and transforms them for its own purposes. Thus soul—pure, immortal, "its essence lily-white ever since Plato"—becomes for the "soul brothers" black, violent, orgiastic; and black, traditionally the color of evil, becomes beautiful. Obscenity is thus used to uncover the pretensions and debase the image of the establishment. "If, for example, the highest executives of the nation or of the state are called, not President X or Governor Y but pig X or pig Y, and if what they say in campaign speeches is rendered as 'oink, oink,' this offensive designation is used to deprive them of the aura of public servants or leaders who have only the common interest in mind."

She found the intensity of movement work exhilarating. Solidarity with others and a new and stronger identification with black people made her increasingly confident of herself and her aims.

Her major activity at San Diego was to spearhead a campaign to turn the then proposed third college into a "Third World College" institution that would be organized around the needs and activities of the black and Chicano academic and local communities. Lumumba Zapata was the name chosen for the new college—the black revolutionary and the Chicano were to be the symbols of its goals. Angela worked out the details of this plan and was chosen to present the written proposal to the Chancellor. "I did not lead the struggle in the sense that there were no other leaders. I must admit that I did play a leading role; but I would not want to underestimate all the contributions—some greater than mine, some less—without which the movement would never have started." When she finally reached the Chancellor, he found Angela "filled with hate." She comments: "Filled with hate? Hate had absolutely nothing to do with it —the man flatters himself when he thinks that we would waste important energies on hating him and his cohorts. We were just extremely serious about our insistence that the university come to grips with its own racism."

There were personal contacts too at San Diego. One of Angela's friends there, a graduate student named Sidney Glass, claims she began to open up almost visibly. "It was a beautiful experience," he says. "At first she thought I was a freshman and I thought she was ugly and coming on too hard. Before I met her, some of the brothers were talking about Angela—that she was trying to make everybody into a Marxist-Leninist. She wasn't ever dogmatic. Wow, I thought, this chick has a good head. But she's in a political box (which was really where I was)." She worked hard; people around not only respected her, they often felt in awe of her; some found her discipline inspirational. And she had her foibles—very human ones. She couldn't take criticism well; the only way she could cope with it was to produce a series of rationalizations within an intellectual framework. She was very hard put to admit she was wrong. "She could also be imperious at times," Sidney Glass said. "Both she and Fania could; they often seemed unconscious of their effect on people." Angela could, however, relax to a more ordinary level at times, and the more she loosened up, the more attractive she became. "Some of the brothers said to her, 'Hey, take off your glasses and get some new rags,'" says Sidney.

In half a dozen different ways California was a water-shed for Angela: it brought her into active constructive campaigning; it put her on platforms as a public speaker; it injected into her almost exclusively academic life large doses of ordinary people and their concerns. And, more important than any of these things, it marked her wholehearted commitment to her people.

By the time she arrived in San Diego, Angela was a convinced Marxist, accepting theoretically at any rate the desirability of the socialist revolution and, *vide* Marcuse, the role of the university in promoting it. But like thousands of other young radical academics, she had not got beyond intellectual conviction to the point of actually working for that revolution. The practical lessons of Frankfurt and of organizing with Stokely Carmichael in London had sunk in, however, and from the moment of arriving in California she had looked for a way to apply them. Naturally she found it among the blacks.

But Angela was not to become exclusively black in her allegiance, a fact that aroused some black antagonism toward her. Rejecting Carmichael's wholehearted separatism, she continued to see the black struggle as part of the larger anti-capitalist struggle while devoting her own time and energies to the cause that was not only most available and nearest to her heart but in which she felt she could be most useful. Now was the time to start paying, in whatever way she could, for all those privileges that one after the other had deposited her high up the American social ladder. Without a doubt her moral and political convictions, her racial allegiance, and her personal fulfillment were all served by the extracurricular work she did with and among the blacks of California.

And then, in the summer of 1968, she joined the Communist Party.

11/A POLITICAL COMMITMENT:
THE CHE LUMUMBA CLUB

"Membership in the Communist Party is a white obsession
—it's an abstraction for black people, or irrelvant."

—BOB SINGLETON

In 1967, at a conference sponsored by the Student non-
violent Coordinating Committee (SNCC) in Los Angeles
Angela met Franklin and Kendra Alexander. They took her
to her first meeting of the Che Lumumba Club of the Communist Party. She began spending much of her time with
them, and with Franklin's sister Charlene Mitchell. Later,
she met Franklin and Charlene's brother, Deacon Alexander,
and she went out with him for many months.

If Angela had formed early sentimental attachments
to the Communist Party through her parents' friends who
were Communists in the South, the Alexanders had practically been born into it. Their father had joined the Party in
Chicago in the 1940s. Charlene Mitchell, a serenely lovely
looking woman, joined in the late 1940s and in 1968 became
the first Communist Party candidate for President since the
Depression. Mrs. Mitchell speaks with affection of Angela
and with even greater conviction about her role in the fight
for Angela's freedom. It was Charlene Mitchell who led the
first all black Communist group—the Che Lumumba Club.
Angela attended the first meeting.

Franklin Delano Alexander, a very tall, imposing man
with an assured manner, has a deep voice which, during
Angela's pre-trial hearings in 1971, rang out in court where

he played a kind of ombudsman—always on the lookout for a hint of injustice. Bob Singleton of UCLA describes Franklin Alexander as a man of almost inhuman integrity. Franklin, though, confesses smilingly to a very human passion for cooking. As the national Chairman of the DuBois Clubs, he proved his organizational skills. His wife Kendra—tall and proud—also belongs to the Communist Party.

In February 1968 Angela moved to Los Angeles while continuing her studies at San Diego. She spent much time in her old blue Rambler hurrying back and forth on the freeway. Neither she nor Deacon Alexander, whom she had begun to see (and continued to see until the fall of 1969), had yet joined the Party. For a time Angela worked in US, an extremist nationalist organization, but she found its ideological stand and its chauvinist views of women unacceptable. Her own attitude is that women's liberation is a vital part of the socialist revolution, that the women's movement must school itself in socialist consciousness and forge its practices accordingly; that "in this way the women's liberation movement may assume its well-earned and unique place among the current gravediggers of capitalism."

At about this time Franklin Alexander began organizing the Black Panther Political Party (named after Stokely Carmichael's Black Panther Political Party in Alabama.) But Huey Newton's Black Panther Party for Self-Defense in Oakland had objections—at the very least over titles. Eventually, Angela and the Alexanders went to work for SNCC instead, and their first aim was forming a people's tribunal to try the Los Angeles Police Department in absentia for the shooting of Gregory Clark, a young black. Angela worked very hard. She was diligent, eager to learn, willing to do petty jobs.

At a Communist Party convention in 1968, with the Alexanders, Angela saw the party in action. It was at a time when her Marxism made her emphasize the importance of the class struggle as well as the race struggle. At the convention she was impressed. On June 22, 1968, she joined the Communist Party, and so did Deacon Alexander. For a time, too, she worked with the Black Panthers, but soon discontinued her efforts for it—for reasons she does not mention. Her real commitment was to the Party, especially to the Che Lumumba Club.

Angela's life was becoming more and more integrated: the people she worked most closely with were also the people she had grown closest to. And these people were black. She had, in a sense, come home.

Few facts about Angela Davis have provoked more anxious questions and unlikely answers than her membership in the Communist Party. And indeed among the young Western radicals of her generation, so unimpressed by the claims of the Socialist countries to be leading any revolution anywhere, it does seem an improbable development. In America, as in France, Germany, and Italy, the young disciples of Marcuse, himself a prestigious critic of Soviet Russia, are invariably at loggerheads with orthodox Communism. They are never within its ranks.

But in fact the puzzle of Angela's Communism is easily solved.

Identification with the Communist Party was the strongest, most challenging commitment Angela could make in America. To be a Communist in America is to be the enemy. It is easier to be a Maoist, a Trotskyite, almost easier to be a Black Panther. Hardly anyone in California knows what the first two are and the last hasn't been around long enough to have acquired the sinister, all-pervasive reputation of the Red. To be a Communist in America so firmly establishes one on the "other side" that just as a gesture it is important. It is a supremely defiant act.

But she had better reasons for taking out a Party card than a mere wish to thumb her nose at the establishment. She was predisposed by childhood contact and sentimental association to think positively of the Communists, but more practically, the Party in California had impressed her with its effectiveness. By 1968 Angela knew her way around a variety of revolutionary (or potentially revolutionary) groups, and had some standards of comparison. She had come to understand that it takes more than a loose organization of likeminded people to produce a serious revolution. It takes planning; even a certain amount of bureaucracy may be involved. And it takes a political party with the means and membership to organize. "According to Angela," Marcuse says, "the Communist Party is the only organization that does anything."

The real significance of her membership, however, is to be found in the part of the Party she chose to join: the Che Lumumba All-Black Collective of the Communist Party of Southern California. Here was an organization focused away from the Soviet Union and onto the Third World, an organization whose international contacts with revolutionary movements in Africa and Latin America fitted in with Angela's own enthusiasm for Cuba, Algeria, and Vietnam. And moreover it was for blacks alone—something the Communist Party of America had been reluctant to permit until the growth of black radicalism persuaded it to think again. On their own initiative, blacks drew what they wanted from the Party. In the case of the Che Lumumba Club, they made it their own. Effective, theoretically rigorous, dynamic, the Communist Party seemed to her the fittest organization in which to carry on the long, slow, difficult struggle to improve conditions for blacks—as for other racial minorities in white-dominated capitalist America.

Angela's commitment was twofold: it was to socialism and it was to her own people. For after the years of being accepted to live, study, work, and compete with whites, she had come to feel as an adult an overriding need to identify with black America and make its fight her own. That she chose to make her commitment in the context of the Communist Party indicates a hardheaded practicality, a long-range willingness to deal with the way she saw reality. Without much chance of approval from intellectual radicals of her own sort, she chose what seemed the most sensible course of action. She explains:

> My decision to join the Che Lumumba Club, a militant all-black collective of the Communist Party, flowed directly from the belief that the only path of liberation for black people is that which leads toward complete and radical overthrow of the capitalist class and all its various instruments of suppression. The Che Lumumba Club is concerned with the task of organizing black people around their immediate needs, but at the same time of creating an army of freedom fighters which will overthrow our enemies. We realize that in order to accomplish this latter goal, we must work in harmony with the progressive forces in America who have seen the nature of the beast.

Its aims are "to organize and teach in specific communities, to promote ties with revolutionary socialism in other countries, to emphasize the national character of the struggle of black people." When Angela joined, it was working toward these targets by organizing groups in hospitals and schools and by running political education classes.

In spite of its self-consciously all-black title, it offered her the opportunity to work with whites as well, both those in other sections of the CPUSA and those in radical organizations with which the Che Lumumba Club joined forces on specific issues.

Both politically and emotionally it was difficult for

Angela to reject all whites, to throw away friendships that had long been important to her, to deny so much of her own past. Politically she knew it was impossible to achieve revolution without combining forces. Marcuse provides an insight here: "If Angela labored under one difficulty—one which some black leaders perhaps strengthened—it was being made to feel she was too much committed to the white establishment. But she wasn't. If you knew her, you couldn't divide, wouldn't imagine her dividing, her world into black and white, for it was from the white world that she drew much of her education and she had many friendships in it." Elfie Hieber, Angela's neighbor at the Factory in Frankfurt, came to visit California in 1968. She remembers painful conflicts with other black radicals over Angela's determination to work with white progressive forces.

Elfie wondered whether some of the attacks against Angela were not really directed against herself; not everyone, she felt, approved of a white person's being welcomed. She sensed a sort of racism from the other side and she—and, she thinks, Angela—found it disturbing. Angela was not aware of any attacks on Elfie, and is sure that none came from her friends. Elfie also saw that Angela was criticized from time to time on other grounds as well: people said to her you have never lived in the ghetto, you haven't had a bad time like us, you always have white friends, and you aren't even completely black. Just at that time, however, Stokely Carmichael spoke at a rally; for the first time he indicated that Left-wing whites might possibly have something to say. Angela was very happy about it, Elfie remembers; she felt it was progress. What really impressed Elfie Hieber was that Angela never for a moment gave up, never once resigned herself, saying, "Well, that's the way it is; there is nothing I can do about the society that made me this way." She had intellectually realized her own problems,

political, personal, and social, and was succeeding in organizing her life accordingly.

Elfie had last seen Angela in 1967. Now in California
she was utterly amazed at the differences she found in her
old friend. Her problems over work, her personal life, and
her future had, perhaps with the help of psychoanalysis,
begun to resolve themselves in Frankfurt. Still, Elfie's
memory was of a fairly frantic person leading a disordered
life, but when she arrived at the Los. Angeles airport, Angela
was there on time to meet her. She took Elfie home. Elfie
exclaims, "There was this little house, very nice, and there
were rooms and there was food in the house; they were cooking and there was dinner ready—everything just as perfect
as you'd expect in a German household. Angela said, 'It certainly isn't like Frankfurt!' and she seemed quite proud of
it." It was indeed very different, Elfie says. There was a har-
monious sense in California, a feeling that Angela was doing
things, not rushing to do them, but accomplishing a great
deal. Angela had just joined the Communist Party; she was
studying ten hours a day for her Ph.D. qualifying exams; she
hadn't yet found a job for the following year. Yet she was
much happier. There was almost nothing left of the tense
person she had been. Although little was said about it, Elfie
let it be understood she had noticed and it was obvious
Angela was pleased.

After Elfie's visit Angela passed her qualifying examinations. By spring of 1969 she was beginning work on her
dissertation. Her political activities continued. She worked
hard; she enjoyed herself. It was a full time. She touched
and was touched by the people around her. She belonged
where she was—personally, politically, intellectually. Then
offers of jobs came from Swarthmore and Yale. Mrs. Davis,
who had trepidations about the California job, encouraged
her daughter to take a job in the East. She didn't much care

for the attitude of California toward young radicals. She was not a little afraid for Angela, who, however, was determined to stay on the West Coast.

A call came in March. It was from Donald Kalish, Chairman of the Department of Philosophy at UCLA. Angela met Professor Kalish, liked him and liked the others she met in his department. Hesitating, she considered the move. She wanted badly to get on with her dissertation; UCLA informed her she could spend the first quarter there at work on her thesis and with no teaching duties. She reconsidered and accepted. Soon after she was hired.

Not long before she went to Cuba on vacation, in June of 1969, someone sent her a copy of the *Daily Bruin*, UCLA's student newspaper. It contained an item of news to the effect that the Philosophy Department had recently hired an instructor who was also a member of the Communist Party. Angela read the *Bruin* article and she laughed. She laughed but, half serious, she said to a friend, "Gosh, I wonder what that means?"

PART V/THE MAKING
OF A CAUSE

"The shoulders of the unveiled Algerian woman are thrust back with easy freedom. She walks with a graceful, measured stride, neither too fast nor too slow. Her legs are bare, not confined by the veil, given back to themselves, and her hips are free."

—Frantz Fanon

Fanon might have been describing Angela as she walked across the UCLA campus. It was the public Angela; she had become a celebrity. She moved both with natural dignity and grace and with an acquired sense of what she had become in the public eye. Angela Davis—her case and the controversy it fired—changed the face of the campus.

UCLA is basically a commuter college. Served by the endless configuration of freeways on which Los Angeles is run and which run it, the university seems an appropriate outgrowth of that motorized city. The approach to the campus is not hospitable. A set of circuitous roads leading from the freeway wind around it. There are innumerable kiosks at which one must request a parking space. There are no illegal places to park. A complex and ingenious system of barricades and coin slots forbids it. Like certain well-run railroad stations in Germany, everything is very efficient if one stays within the designated boundaries. One leaves the ugly concrete parking structures with endless rows of cars baking in the sun and the picture changes as rapidly as if someone had changed the slide in a projector. Green and pretty, the campus is dotted with unhurried, unworried students. Between classes scores of students swarm from building to building as if someone had unplugged the classrooms. The bell sounds, they disappear. The campus gives itself up to the sun again, a 1940s college musical with only miniskirts, an occasional beard, and a soaring frisbee to update it.

With the Angela Davis Case, the UCLA campus began to shed its reputation as the most complacent, least political branch of the California system whose students come to class during the day only to return to their real lives at night. When Angela walked across the perfectly green lawns, people stared. Many smiled or waved a clenched fist in support and admiration. A few glared with hatred. Angela was a unique and striking figure. She had taken a stand, openly admitted her Communist affiliation, been fired, rehired, tested, idolized, and symbolized. She never faltered and the effect on the university as well as the rest of the country was enormous. The price she paid was becoming a cause.

Then came the *Daily Bruin* article. In it the writer, William Tulio Divale, a graduate student in anthropology, wrote: "The Philosophy Department has recently made a two-year appointment of an Acting Assistant Professor. The person is well-qualified for the post and is also a member of the Communist Party."

Unimpressed by this scoop, the world minded its own affairs for the best part of six weeks, until Ed Montgomery published a piece in the *San Francisco Examiner* on July 9, revealing that the person alluded to in the *Bruin* was a known Maoist who, according to U.S. Intelligence reports, had been active in the SDS and the Black Panthers.

An interesting fact came to light about Bill Divale soon after he exposed Angela Davis. Not only was Divale a graduate student at UCLA, he was also a paid informer for the FBI. What he began at UCLA eventually invited far more interest than he had ever imagined.

Most people assumed that Ed Montgomery had picked

up the information about Angela from Divale's article. Montgomery denies this, claiming that his special interest in the Black Panthers had put him on to her long before. Montgomery, it seems, had been keeping tabs on Angela for quite a while. He tells his story willingly. A large, jovial loose-limbed man, at ease behind his desk, in a short-sleeved nylon shirt, he grins often and talks with as much sincerity as fluency, stopping only to "change the baby"—a tiny battery in his hearing aid.

He claims he got a lead on Angela from a San Diego friend whose daughter attended lectures at UCSD given by a teaching assistant named Angela Davis. The daughter informed her father that Miss Davis was teaching "radical ideas" in class. The father informed his reporter friend, Ed Montgomery, and Montgomery thought it proper to inform the world. First, though, he picked up the phone, called Angela at her apartment at Cardiff-by-the-Sea near La Jolla, and inquired if she belonged to the Communist Party. Politely she replied that she did. He pressed her for information about her relationship with the Black Panthers, but she "clammed up." Montgomery turned his attention to Professor Kalish.

Using his wide range of contacts inside the FBI and the various California police departments, he assembled a lengthy dossier on Kalish. Kalish not only had a "long record of radical activity," he was "buddies" with Irving Sarnoff, a "longtime member of the Communist Party." Both men were tied in with the Los Angeles Peace Council, which Ed Montgomery considers highly subversive. One incident stuck in Montgomery's mind.

It seems that in 1968 Donald Kalish was responsible for the anti-Vietnam War "disturbances" when President Johnson visited Los Angeles. During a riot on the Avenue of the Stars, a young woman broke through police lines yelling, "The President killed my brother in Vietnam." Arrested, the girl confessed the "truth." She had, it seems, been picked up one afternoon in front of Saks Fifth Avenue in Beverly Hills. From there she was taken to "Party Headquarters" and "coached" on how to act. The man who picked her up that day was none other than Donald Kalish. The very same Kalish who took part in subversive activity. The very same Professor Kalish who, in the spring of 1969, hired Angela Davis to teach at UCLA. So much for the Montgomery story, researched in the eager hunt for some sort of "Communist conspiracy" behind Angela's move to UCLA.

Professor Kalish, a voluble, hyperactive man with great charm and intelligent eyes, has a different version of the Montgomery "story": the girl who "confessed" to police that Kalish had brainwashed her was an agent from the very start. Coached by the FBI to contact Kalish, she called him with a story about her brother killed in Vietnam. How could she help? she begged, nearly in tears. Kalish asked if she wanted to take part in the upcoming rally against the war. Agreeing, she worked her way into the organizing committee.

Even after Montgomery's "exposure" of Angela, the public remained largely indifferent. But the two articles, Montgomery's and Divale's, set off an extraordinary chain of events, events that at first seemed no more than routine academic red tape. But it was with them that the Angela Davis Case really began. It was the moment when the person was turned into a symbol, a heroine, a cause, and subsequently victim, martyr, or murderer, depending on one's point of view. These small, dull events when tied together ignited a slow-burning fuse. The end result was explosive.

The case at UCLA and that at San Rafael were to prove inextricably intertwined. They were to be neither separate nor separable, related to each other and both related to the affair of the Soledad Brothers, and to the questions of political freedom, racism, and justice under California law. The State of California and its university are ruled by the same system of laws; the Governor of the state is also head of the Board of Regents and, as such, he rules the university. Under these laws Angela was fired from her job because of her political affiliation, accused of murder, indicted, imprisoned. Thus a description of the way various rules and laws were invoked and set into action against her tells a good deal about California, its university, its bureaucracy, and its attitudes.

The facts that led up to Angela's dismissal go back to March of 1969, when she was still at San Diego. They appear innocent enough. Chronologically it all began when Donald Kalish heard about Angela from Princeton's Philosophy Department chairman, who, while impressed, felt her not quite suitable. Kalish called her at San Diego. She went for an interview at UCLA and everything proceeded in a perfectly ordinary manner. "To be serious, I really had no idea that there would be the type of reaction there was to my being a Communist," Angela told me later. "I knew there would be something because when anyone has been intensely involved in political things and becomes a professor, he's subjected to some forms of harassment, but I never expected this. I didn't know Kalish at all. He called me at school one day and asked if I'd be interested in a job at UCLA. There were interviews, I met with the department, they decided to hire me. I talked about the fact that I was politically involved—I didn't see the necessity of mentioning the fact that I was a member of the Communist Party. But I'd never made a secret of it at San Diego."

Kalish felt that Angela's academic record made up for the fact that she was not trained in analytic philosophy as was most of the department. For this reason some members of the department voted against her. Kalish, however, supported her, and for the very reason that she offered a different background, the administration approved the appointment and signed after three days. Angela received a letter that read, "The appointment is intended for two years. The question of a continued (*i.e.*, permanent) position at UCLA beyond the second year is left open now and will be considered while you are here."

That summer when Kalish met Angela at a meeting of the United Front Against Fascism in Oakland, she said, "I'll be cutting cane in Cuba this summer. I wanted to let you know." For the first time Kalish considered that she might be a Communist.

At the time Angela was hired department chairmen had control over the hiring and firing of nontenured personnel. There remained, after Professor Kalish invited her to join the faculty, only a number of formalities to complete and some employment forms to be signed. The key to what happened was, as Kalish puts it, that "although no appointment had ever been handled so quickly," the employment form covering the summer quarter reached the office only *after it was known* she was a Communist—a discovery that caused a total reversal of opinion in the administration.

"Summer supplements" are not intrinsically interesting except to the University of California teacher who receives the fee for the one quarter in four he does not teach. In Angela's case this minor technicality gave the administration (on orders from the Board of Regents) a hook on which to hang her eventual dismissal. On April 21, 1969, she was offered as part of her job a 2/9 salary supplement for her "off quarter" each year—to take effect from that summer of 1969. The Vice-Chancellor authorized the supplement; the Office of the Dean authorized it. But though it was submitted to the administration by the Philosophy Department, the "change of employment" form was never signed. Angela was never paid for the summer.

Meanwhile, quite apart from Angela's appointment, the university was taking a stand on the intrusion of politics into hiring and firing. No doubt the controversies over Marcuse, Eldridge Cleaver, and others had alerted academics to the dangers posed by their reactionary masters.

On June 2 the Faculty Senate issued a statement warning all campus agencies to avoid any "implicit or explicit self-censorship which permits the questioning of the political acceptability of candidates to intrude itself in the review process." At the end of the month, under pressure from the faculty, the Regents of the university reaffirmed an earlier ruling by issuing an order that read, "No political test shall ever be considered in the appointment and promotion of any faculty member or employee." This applied to everyone in the university, but in any case it was not the Regents but the department chairmen who were responsible for employing junior faculty members (like Angela).

Around July 16 someone in the Regents' office happened to notice the Divale and Montgomery articles. The Regents were quickly informed and they in turn directed the Chancellor's Office at UCLA to obtain the "necessary information." No contracts were to be signed before information on Angela Davis' affiliation with the Communist Party was in hand. Complying with the Regents' demands, the Chancellor's Office sent Angela a letter on July 25.

All this while Angela was in Cuba on a working vacation. "Havana is pretty much like any city, but when you get out in the country it's entirely different. Everyone's very poor, very friendly. People stop to talk or invite you home. I cut cane, discussed everything with the Cubans—workers, students, party leaders. The Cuban experience was enlightening." She recognized more clearly than ever the necessity of organization to effect a revolution that would be more than theory, fantasy, or an exciting moment of direct action: "I think the brother in *Battle of Algiers*," she said later in an interview in jail, "was unquestionably correct when he contended that although a revolution is hard to initiate and although it is even harder to sustain to the point of seizing power, the most difficult period of all is the building of the revolutionary society after the seizure of power." When Angela left Cuba that August, she looked forward to going back in the summer of 1970 to learn more about the country and its people.

Back at UCLA, the Chancellor's Office discovered that the "change in employment" form granting a summer supplement was, to their great relief, still unsigned. Without that signature it was just possible to conceive of Angela's contract as incomplete. The administration had found its loophole. It is not impossible that in their anxiety not to be labeled "soft on Communism," the Regents were keeping at least one eye open for just such an issue as this. In any case, they were not going to let it go when it arrived literally on their doorstep. They instructed their lawyer to inform the Philosophy Department that while the 1940, 1949, and 1950 resolutions barring Communist Party members from teaching had been declared constitutionally invalid, the Regents meant to force a ruling through the courts again. If Angela won, at least the Regents could not be held responsible for letting a Communist loose on the campus. If the Regents won, they would receive accolades from many grateful citizens. Still out of town and unaware of these machinations, Angela was becoming the pawn in a giant academic-political match.

Returning to Los Angeles on September 5, she found a copy of the letter from the Chancellor's Office demanding to know whether she belonged to the Communist Party. After considerable thought she replied, "The question posed by Mr. Saxon [the Vice-Chancellor] is impermissible. This on grounds of constitutional freedom as well as academic policy. . . . You are without authority to require an answer concerning mere membership in the Communist Party or to deprive me of employment on such grounds." The letter concluded with the statement in which Angela put herself on the line:

> However, and without waiving my objections to the question posed, my answer is that I am now a member of the Communist Party. While I think this membership requires no justification, I want you to know that as a black woman, I feel an urgent need to find radical solutions to the problems of racial and national minorities in the white capitalist United States. I feel that my membership in the Communist Party has widened my horizons and expanded my opportunities for perceiving such solutions and working for their effectuation. The problems to which I refer have lasted too long and wreaked devastation too appalling to permit complacency or half measures in their resolution. It goes without saying, of course, that advocacy of the Communist Party during my period of membership in it has, to my knowledge, fallen well within the guarantees of the First Amendment. Nor does my membership in the Communist Party involve me in any commitment to principles or positions, governing either my scholarship or my responsibilities as a teacher. I am unable to regard Mr. Saxon's inquiry of 16 July 1969 as unrelated to the fact that I have not received the summer stipend which I was to receive beginning August 1, 1969, as part of my contract of employment with the university.

Since my membership in the Communist Party is irrelevant to my qualifications and appointment as an Acting Assistant Professor, it is equally irrelevant to my eligibility for receipt of the summer stipend. I am advised that the university has duly entered into a legal obligation in this respect, and I should greatly appreciate receipt of the agreed upon sums. The failure to receive it has already occasioned some hardship.

This subtle and carefully calculated letter, while providing the information asked for, attempted to challenge the use that would be made of that information, answering charges not yet made. Clearly Angela understood the implications of the Chancellor's interest in her politics and of the nonpayment of her stipend.

Then the bomb exploded: on September 19, 1969, the Regents of the university adopted a resolution calling on University President Charles Hitch to end Professor Davis' appointment, citing in support of their decision the anti-Red resolutions of 1940, 1949, and 1950. On September 22 Angela received a letter stating that her contract would be terminated immediately unless she submitted to a hearing, which she subsequently did, only to find it a meaningless formality. So between March and September of 1969 she had been interviewed, hired, investigated by the FBI, exposed by reporter Ed Montgomery, reviewed by the Regents, and fired according to resolutions judged illegal by the courts. She had never taught a single class.

The Philosophy Department went quietly about its business. Angela had not been assigned to teach in the fall quarter, but Kalish asked Angela if she would like to take over a course, "Recurring Philosophical Themes in Black Literature," for which there was no teacher. Anxious to demonstrate her competence and to refute charges that she would indoctrinate students, she accepted. The quarter began.

On October 1 the UCLA Academic Senate voted their disapproval of the Regents' stand. Chancellor Charles Young backed them, but he still hesitated to sign Angela's contract. Caught between desire for approbation from the academic community and the power the Regents held, Young was to become the man in the middle. On October 3 a taxpayers' suit against the Regents was filed by members of the Philosophy Department and the Law School. To head off the tempest (they thought) the Regents took a precedent-setting stand by allowing Professor Davis to teach—but without credit. No student would receive credit for enrolling in her course. This move—the denial of status, especially to a black woman—plus the failure to find academic grounds for dismissal boomeranged on the Regents.

Professor Davis taught her first class in the biggest auditorium on campus to a packed house. Two weeks later, on October 20, Los Angeles Superior Court Judge Jerome Pacht enjoined the Regents to spend no more money on ousting Angela Davis. According to Judge Pacht, the contrived hearings on her dismissal were improper and the antiquated anti-Communist rulings unconstitutional. The Chancellor was forced to restore credit. As usual, the Regents had a legal loophole to crawl through. Arguing that the true corporate home of the university was Alameda County in northern California, they insisted that one suit should be reheard there, and they won their point on December 23. The original ruling had, however, another sixty days to run. The plaintiffs in the taxpayers' suit (Angela's case) petitioned the California Supreme Court on the change of venue issue and a hearing was granted, delaying the whole matter until June 1970. Angela's position as a teacher therefore remained legal.

What made everything more confusing, if possible, was that all this litigation technically had nothing to do with Angela's contract for the following year (1970–71). Renewal hearings in a case like hers (reappointment for a second year) are generally a formality. In this instance they became a major issue. Feeling they were defeated in the courts, this same Board of Regents decided to put the pressure on in the matter of her continued employment—something normally the preserve of the faculty alone. In effect, Angela was continually on trial before both court and university administration through the year. It left little time for her own work. Without sufficient progress on her doctoral thesis there could be a real reason to question her renewal. These pressures alone would have been enough for anyone to handle. But she was to be subjected to many more. Angela had become a cause.

13 / ON CAMPUS, FOR CREDIT, AS PLANNED

"To the black community, the students will make up the cadres who will assume important roles in leading a people determined to make their own destinies. To be out of touch with them is to lose them in the future. If we may speak figuratively, the University of California sits on a bomb. Those with responsibility for its affairs hold the match. Professor Davis is the fuse."

—Bob Singleton

"I had the delight of meeting her the first day she came to UCLA," says Bob Singleton. "We got her to come and have dinner with a bunch of us. She was such a nice person, she laughed so well, she was so obviously relaxed and glad to see some black people and talk about things." Bob Singleton was co-head of UCLA's Afro Studies Program, and he met her at a quiet point in her life. Her objective then was to finish her thesis, and he believes she would have done just that if "the Regents hadn't blown the whistle." Everyone was taken by her intelligence, her style, her looks. Over the months she was to grow tense, to laugh less and less. But that first evening, Bob recalls, "there was the warm feeling you get when a person that bright turns out to be beautiful as well and has everything else going for her."

ON CAMPUS FOR CREDIT AS PLANNED read the buttons that popped up all over campus when Angela taught her first class in October. Thousands, including all those enrolled in her course, turned out to show support for her. The buttons were flown down from Berkeley, where they had already seen use in the previous year's controversy over Eldridge Cleaver's right to teach there.

"Teaching isn't just standing up in front of a class

spouting some sort of truths, but a learning process on both sides," Angela told me. Her students were willing to learn and they liked her; she liked them and enjoyed teaching. Donald Kalish noted the warmth and rapport between his new assistant professor and her students and colleagues: "She became distinctive because she quickly became someone the black students identified with. She didn't Uncle Tom the establishment. The black faculty felt an extra need to get behind her. For students she was a model of what a teacher should be—young, involved, willing to fight, and highly intelligent. She was altogether extraordinary."

Though she seemed self-assured in the classroom, her public presence was in fact something acquired slowly and not without some emotional pain. Haunted by sensation-hunters, reporters following her for a "juicy detail," people who just wanted to get a look, she tried not to show anger or resentment, but was polite to everyone. Unable to escape the role thrust upon her, she played it as well as she could, helped not only by her beliefs, but by the knowledge that she looked attractive and moved with grace. She dressed well; her years in Europe had given her a certain style. She grimaced at the ugly photographs of herself and was eager to see some better ones. The press, she said wryly, had the habit of photographing her in poses that made her look monstrous: mouth open, eyes feverish, arms outstretched. The first time she spoke in public at the vast UCLA stadium she wore a string of beads. Nervously, she pulled at the necklace until it slid and tightened around her throat. The resulting pictures made her seem to be strangling herself.

Over the months she learned to control her nervousness in public and on television. She learned to articulate well, to talk deliberately, to think on her feet. "I never once saw her tongue outrun her brain," Bob Singleton recalls. On the surface she seemed a streamlined performer, but underneath she was still "a little girl building the emotional ability to do it, very afraid of being left alone." Angela coped with this difficult situation by separating it from herself. Her problems with the Regents weren't just a private quarrel but a skirmish in the black liberation struggle; the charismatic leader was a role she had to play. At times, Bob Singleton remembers, she visibly relaxed into her own private personality, as if taking off a mask that had become stifling. "After a brilliant speech which would have blown anyone's mind, she'd turn to you and ask, 'Did I say that right?' "

Her sense of the ridiculous helped. With some glee she told me about the evening she'd been invited to translate for Jean Genet at a large reception. A pudgy middle-aged Los Angeles matron, blinking coyly, asked her to tell Genet how much she adored and admired him. With an almost straight face, Angela repeated the compliments in French. "*Sans espoir*," came Genet's answer. "You haven't got a chance," Angela told the woman. Then there was the reporter who was always so concerned about Angela's alleged sexiness and her wardrobe: he complained to her about student vigilantes peering over his shoulder while he made notes on her "costume" for "background color" in class that morning. "That's good," Angela grinned, "the students are on their job."

She too was on her job and that meant far more than seeing reporters or going to receptions. Her office was cluttered with books in German and French and English, with stacks of notes for her thesis, class lists, and memos from her lawyers. Coffee cups and half-eaten sandwiches, candy wrappers and cigarette butts littered a long table. Peanuts and chocolate milk were often the only lunch she got. Posters of Eldridge Cleaver and Bobby Seale hung on the wall. On the blackboard she had chalked a poem by black Cuban poet Nicolas Gullen:

How To Become a Southern Governor:

When you have taught your dog
to pounce upon a Black
and nip his guts
for a snack
When you have learned
how to bark
and wag your tail
then be happy
White man
You can be governor
of your state.

The door to her office was always open. Angela sat behind the large desk, talking into the telephone, looking up to welcome friends and students, lighting one Gauloise after the other. Her voice was soft and gentle and a little shy. She hesitated slightly when speaking with someone, as if listening carefully, as if what they said was important enough to absorb before answering. There was a warmth in her eyes and the charm of enthusiasm in her voice. She coped with everything in a cool and thoughtful way, only occasionally looking confused at the morass of paperwork on her desk. The striking thing was her ability to communicate with a vast range of people in a single afternoon. From her lawyer, with whom she discussed the details of her court case, she would turn to a student to talk about grading procedures or listen to plans for a rally. A half hour later she would be off to teach a class in Kantian philosophy, and on the way back she would pass the time of day with a friend or Donald Kalish, who had come along to see how she was. An hour went one day to a middle-aged black woman who needed help with a philosophy course. Angela's change of tone was imperceptible. It bothered the administration that she got across to so many kinds of people; it gave her the sort of power they hadn't reckoned with as they relentlessly pursued their effort to get her off campus.

The Regents had not been smart enough to foresee that reaction to the case would reach monumental proportions. It was not, as cynics suggested, merely losing a job that disturbed Angela and frightened the academic community. It was that major issues were at stake. And the three biggest: academic freedom, free political choice, and racism were all potential high explosives.

When the Regents fired Angela, they took control of what had been a departmental function (the hiring and firing of nontenured faculty). This in itself would have caused at least a mild uproar because it set limits to academic autonomy within the university, making the teacher as dependent as a serf on the uncertain will of the Board. If the Regents, who with few exceptions have no academic qualifications, were given authority to hire and fire, they might soon be writing the syllabus and requiring the inclusion or exclusion of certain courses. In practical terms it scared the nontenured faculty into the realization that they might find themselves in the same precarious position as Angela. Those who had tenure feared encroachment on what they taught and on what they said—in the classroom or out of it. For there was about the Regents' anti-Angela campaign an old, familiar, and unpleasant stink of political oppression. The ancient bogeyman of Communist affiliation was resurrected.

Feeling ran high at UCLA. If the Regents could drag out illegal anti-Communist rulings and use them to dispose of black female scholars, everyone was vulnerable. Many of the young faculty members knew Angela differed from them only in her having joined the Party. Otherwise their views were similar to hers—if not more radical. There was fear that the atmosphere hostile to black scholars was becoming as pervasive as the tear gas lying over many a university compus and drifting into anyone's office in that year of the Cambodia invasion. When the Angela Davis case broke, the faculty issued this statement:

> We are witnessing the beginning of a political purge in the University of California, an attempt to remove or at least silence the University faculty and students who hold liberal views on such problems as the Vietnam war, the militarization of the American government, racism in America, student participation in the university and so on. Who will be next? Someone who opposes atomic testing? Someone in the fight against offshore oil companies who have polluted the Santa Barbara coast? Such purges are the instruments of totalitarian governments. They cannot be tolerated in our free society.

What really fired the issues, though, was the question of race.

"A paternalistic effort to prescribe for the black community a political litmus test." So the Regents' attempt to fire Angela has been summed up. If the issues of academic freedom and free political choice are difficult to separate, it is because they are inseparable. Angela had, in fact, been denied academic freedom as a direct result of her political affiliations. At first it seemed that her Communist Party membership was what provoked reaction, both pro and con. It became increasingly less simple. She was a woman in a time when women were feeling a need to liberate themselves; she was an intellectual in a state run by anti-intellectuals; she was extraordinarily attractive as a human being and as a spokesman for her beliefs. These qualities subjected her variously to criticism and praise by the press, the public, and the academic community. But if she was all these things, there was something more that many saw as the real root of the reaction: Angela was black.

The Regents and the administration tried hard, tried desperately to keep race out of the controversy, but they failed. When they used a black woman to defy the Academic Senate's ruling that political affiliation could not be made the basis for hiring or firing a teacher, they convinced the black community—and others—that racism was the hidden motive. Political tests, it was pointed out, weigh heaviest on minorities, which are most likely to have ideas and views different from and more radical than those of the majority in power. One false step that left the Regents flat on their faces was allowing Angela to teach without credit at the beginning of the year. It looked very much as if they wanted to reduce a black woman to second-class status.

The attitude of the State of California was clear, however, when Max Rafferty, Governor Ronald Reagan's chief of education, responded to the twenty black professors who pledged to withhold grades until credit for Angela's course was restored: "It makes no difference whether they're black, brown, or polka-dotted. The question is, Who's going to run the store? The profs just work there." It made a big difference, however, to those profs, as well as to the students and the local black community. It also made a big difference to Angela. Her own commitment to black causes grew as she saw her own situation reflected in the experiences of other black people.

Teachers, students, even the administration gave her respect for her academic abilities. From the black community there came not only respect but love. She took great satisfaction in this. She had not expected hostility, but she was surprised at how differently black people reacted to the media-made image of her. A "typical bourgeois response was what I expected: I defend you because you're black—dissociating myself entirely from your politics." She found that black people identified with her in a very personal way: "Brothers and sisters I'd meet quite casually going shopping or taking a walk would say things like, 'If the man gets so uptight because you're a Communist, then there must be something good about Communists. After all, they tried to say Martin Luther King was one.' "

Many white liberals who had supported her over academic freedom got could feet, she found, when Angela linked her case to that of Bobby Seale, the Chairman of the Black Panther Party who was then on trial in New Haven. While some of the backing from women's liberation was valuable, she had the occasional feeling that people merely felt impelled to help the "helpless female." But the support, both real and emotional, that came from black people kept her going. Her desire for identification was fulfilled.

There was an old man who recognized Angela one day as she went into a Westwood delicatessen for lunch. He waited politely until she finished eating. Then he came over and shook her hand and said "Congratulations." He understood, not Marx or Marcuse perhaps, but that Angela was black and was standing up for what she believed and that she was very important to him and his children. The man patted her cheek fondly. She blushed a little, thanked him, and smiled.

Just as the Regents had not predicted faculty reaction —or the reaction of the black community—and therefore had no control over it, they were careless of the fact that in dealing with Angela, they were up against someone who plainly meant to fight. They underestimated her strength and her commitment. She wasn't going to run. The UCLA affair shows that the easy copout for Angela would have been to take the Fifth. According to David Poindexter, she said, "I'm going to teach three thousand students and I'm going to teach them damn well!" And Professor Angela Davis did, by all accounts, teach her students damn well. She was so close in age and conscience to many of her students that an occasionally rather magical sense of communication grew up between them in class.

"You have to get education out of the museum," she felt. Years earlier when she first met Marcuse at Brandeis, she had been impressed by him because his approach related philosophy to the changing world. That was the tradition she intended to carry on. The point of education was to discover and respond to human needs, emotionally and practically. Education was political in the widest sense of the word: it responded to pressing problems in a society. "I can't and I won't," she said in her opening lecture on October 8, "keep my political opinions out of the classroom." Concluding that socialism is the only means to eliminate human suffering, she felt it her right to say to her students, "I have given these things a lot of thought. My feeling is that only some form of communism is going to solve our basic problems." She explained, "I want them to think about it, to criticize, to say whether they think I'm right, to present other solutions they feel might be better. This is the process of education—a free atmosphere where everything can be subjected to a critical attitude."

Stimulated to new extravagance by the sinister word "Communist" and realizing that Angela's influence stretched far beyond her classroom doors, the media tried desperately to alter the mantle of Marcuse to fit her. It didn't work: she was too clearly a representative of a new, genuinely American, breed of academic young, involved, committed. Angela went on record to agree with the Regents that her Party membership said "something about the kind of mind I have," and explained, "I don't mean that I received directives from the Party on how to conduct my class . . . or that I would be incapable of free thought. Education is inherently political; it ought to create human beings who use the knowledge they acquire to conquer nature for the purpose of freeing man."

Students as well as faculty members responded well to her frank statement of her views. At first some came to her classes from vague political commitment or from plain curiosity to see the famous "black, brilliant, and sexy" Angela perform. Others came and stayed because they were interested in a very well-taught class. "I've never been so impressed with a professor's organization," said one boy. When she lectured, the hall was crammed. Students sat on the floor or in the aisles. Teaching seemed to come naturally to her. Standing at the lectern, wearing slacks or a casual dress and holding a cigarette—often so intent upon her teaching that she forgot to light it—she talked fluently. Clearly, she was master of her material, whether she was teaching Philosophical Themes in Black Literature in the first quarter, Kant in the winter, or Existentialism in the spring. Question-and-answer periods were noisy and provocative, the students rising well to the challenge to do some thinking for themselves. Her insistence on the practical was noted. One graduate student remarked, "She presents material in an illuminating style, relating it to the contemporary scene without sacrificing either historical accuracy or philosophical rigor. Her rapport with students is very high." A professor who observed her teach reported that although "she was not reluctant to express her own views, especially in response to a direct and relevant question," she never forced her beliefs on anyone. Another graduate student commented, "Miss Davis is objective. A course in dialectical materialism taught by someone sympathetic to this broad position is surely sensible. We do not lack for criticism and even distortion of this view in the university, to say nothing of the coverage by the mass media . . . every professor has something to 'profess' . . . even if it's only a glorification of neutrality. I would much rather know the philosophical and political position held by a professor from the beginning of a course than have to spend weeks uncovering that position by inference." One student did criticize Angela: "She's very fair, but I think Angela Davis and people like her are too idealistic. They look for a society where everyone is going to help everyone else out."

There was no letup from pressures as spring came. Looking back, Angela notes wryly, "As for relaxation, I didn't recognize the name. There wasn't time to relax, except when I took it easy talking to friends, maybe a movie once a month." But she wasn't tempted to retreat from combat: the personal terrors she suffered brought the kind of system she was fighting literally into her own backyard.

Hate mail arrived daily; telephone threats were commonplace. In the spring she was forced to leave her apartment. A fanatic revealed to the LA police that she had tried to force him—through hypnosis—to shoot himself; claiming psychic messages from the beyond, he later tried to run her down with his car. But she continued to teach, to speak in public, to fight her court battles. She was not to be cowed. Bob Singleton, joint leader with Professor Henry McGee of the Angela Davis Defense Committee at UCLA, kept a careful eye on her to see if she would crack under the pressures. Neither Bob nor his colleagues had ever had "the impression that she was any stronger than anyone else, only a lot smarter." Some of the money the committee raised to pay lawyers went for medication. Angela had to be on the alert. She kept on pushing when she should have been in bed asleep, Bob adds. The calls kept coming. Wherever she went the calls followed, threatening she was going to get it. "She would go from place to place, a little afraid of being killed," Bob says. "She never really said the words, but I could see the tension, her eyes darting back and forth; those calls really worked on her. She never told me what people said in so many words but she would almost break down. She'd only turn to me and say, 'Those people don't even know me, why should they want to take my life?' "

14/SPRING 1970: THE FIRING OF ANGELA DAVIS

"They are going to take your job. I know they are—anything else would be expecting too much. They can't, however, stop you from teaching in public institutions, can they?"

—GEORGE JACKSON

By the end of April, Angela felt sure that Chancellor Young would fire her, unable to stand the Regents pressure. The official "Blue Ribbon" committee that Young had appointed had, to the Regents' dismay, reported that Professor Davis was not only suitable and unbiased, but a superlative teacher. Young postponed his decision week after week. If he supported her, he was in trouble with the Board of Regents that, in practical terms, owned him. If he complied with them, he would lose all credibility with faculty and students. Neither Young nor anyone else, however, foresaw what the spring of 1970 would bring.

The tension felt by everyone was something new for UCLA. At Berkeley, wise to the ways of political spring fever, people said, "Don't plan on taking that course this quarter. There never is a spring quarter any more." At UCLA, however, springtime politics meant no more than class elections. The administration tried to head off anything more serious. Referring to Angela and associated irritants, President Hitch said, "The university is to be regarded as neutral. We don't take positions on political issues. I think the public has been misled by some of these things and by the play they are given in the news media. Ninety-nine percent of the time at 99 percent of the colleges, we go about the business of education and lots of it is pretty conventional stuff. . . . In fact we have made a great deal of progress in the last five years. We have more than doubled the size of the university."

Hitch talked of size and progress. That same year the Bank of America burned at Isla Vista. Four students were murdered at Kent State, others were killed at Jackson State. President Nixon announced the invasion of Cambodia and across the country college after college shut down in outrage. President Nixon also tried to discuss football with students on the steps of the Lincoln Memorial at dawn.

As she increasingly came to see her case as a piece of what was happening around her, Angela's commitment to action intensified. She felt that "people talk about supporting the right of a black Communist to teach on this campus. They are hypocritical if they do not also support the right of Black Panthers to organize in the community." By May 15, finally awakened from his semicomatose dithering by the shouts of demonstrators, Chancellor Young announced his decision to rehire Angela. Given the strength of public indignation he had little choice. American troops were dead in Cambodia, American students were dead on campuses; Kingman Brewster, Yale's president, had said that black men had little chance for justice in American courts of law. Still hedging his bets, however, Young did not sign Angela's contract despite face-saving public statements of his decision to do so, but these prevarications did not help him. To the Regents, Young had become a disobedient child, too irresponsible to be allowed to play with power any longer. The Board of Regents took it away from him by releasing this statement: "Resolved: That the Regents hereby relieve the President of the university, the Chancellor of the Los Angeles campus and all other administrative officers of any further authority or responsibility in connection with the reappointment or nonreappointment of Acting Assistant Professor Angela Davis."

This, everyone knew, was the first step toward firing her. Having assumed the authority to do so, all the Regents now needed was a pretext. There were no academic grounds on which to dismiss her; raising the issue of Communism again was too tricky even for this group of subtle political magicians skilled in making university funds and professors appear and disappear almost at will. And Angela was certainly not to be placated or shut up on the issues she was fighting for. Among these was the case of the Soledad Brothers; the speeches she made on their behalf were finally the convenient grounds on which the Regents based her dismissal.

On January 13, 1970, an exercise yard for maximum security prisoners was opened at the Soledad Prison in Salinas, California. Fifteen inmates—a careless, if not an intentionally explosive mixture of militant blacks and racist whites—were thoroughly skin-searched for weapons and allowed outside. Almost at once a fight broke out. The guard in the tower, O. G. Miller, fired into the group of struggling men. He was a crack marksman. At the fourth shot one white convict lay wounded and three black convicts were dead.

Three days later the District Attorney of Monterey County ruled the guard's action justifiable homicide and a grand jury confirmed the verdict. The same day, within half an hour of the announcement over the prison radio, a white guard, John Mills, was beaten and thrown to his death over the jail's third-tier railing. All hundred and thirty-seven convicts in Y wing where the murder happened were confined to their cells. Meeting in secret, the grand jury found sufficient evidence to indict three blacks for murder: Fleeta Drumgo,

John Clutchette, and George Jackson. The three men were to become famous as the Soledad Brothers.

The evidence against the Soledad Brothers was not substantial: no inmate of Y wing on the day John Mills was killed there had been involved in the incident in the exercise yard. But the three were known militants. This was enough for the prison authorities: only the militants could have organized the revenge. Still in the strictest secrecy, two hearings on the charge had already been held before John Clutchette contrived to smuggle out word of what was happening. Thereafter the case of the Soledad Brothers raged with the power and fury of a forest fire through the ranks of the radicals.

At the center of the campaign was a defense committee, hiring lawyers, working out legal tactics, raising funds, organizing protest meetings, putting out propaganda, and above all, turning the spotlight of maximum publicity on the sinister goings-on in Soledad. From the beginning Angela was in it and was soon the committee's Los Angeles co-chairman. Along with the rest of the world she learned that John Clutchette was twenty-three, Fleeta Drumgo twenty-four, George Jackson twenty-six; that Jackson had been sentenced to jail for one year to life at the age of seventeen when he pleaded guilty (at the request of a state anxious to save court costs) to a seventy-dollar holdup at a gas station; that in jail ever since, he had spent seven years in solitary confinement. If anything was ever worth fighting for, this was it—this horrendous example of the oppression white capitalist America inflicted on its blacks. Her own grievance against the university Regents began to rate pretty low in the injustice stakes.

Angela threw everything she had into the Soledad Brothers' defense campaign, and by now she had plenty. She had belief, passion, and training. She had participated in other campaigns to free other prisoners. It was as if all her experiences since reaching California had been getting her into shape for this work, preparing her for public performance in the Soledad Brothers' cause. Now she was direct, effective, powerful; able to dominate an enormous rally, to sway thousands; a beautiful, terrible symbol of outrage.

But she also worked in private, meeting the parents, friends, lawyers of the accused to learn from them how best she could help, discussing what should be done. She met George Jackson's younger brother, Jonathan, then seventeen, an intelligent, articulate boy for whom his brother's predicament overrode every other thought. With Georgia Jackson (George's mother), his sister Penny, and her own sister Fania, Angela went to a meeting at Pasadena one night and from there to the Jackson home. Wakened by their arrival, Jonathan got up and joined them, to argue for hours about the pros and cons of political agitation. "I loved Jonathan very deeply," Angela said later. "He was extremely perceptive—far older than his years—and I found him to be very helpful in a lot of things." One practical way in which Jonathan Jackson was helpful was in bodyguarding Angela against the threats of her enemies.

And then, one day in May 1970, she walked into the Salinas courtroom and met George Jackson. There had been no more important meeting in her life.

George Jackson had fifteen more months to live when he and Angela first saw each other. Outside of the courtroom they met only once—and that was in jail. Yet through the concrete of Soledad (and later San Quentin) and across the distance that separated his imprisonment from her liberty, and later, across the distance between their respective cells in two separate prisons, a profoundly fullling relationship developed between them. Something of the depth and intensity of what they felt can be grasped from their letters to each other. These letters show that, for Angela, George Jackson perfectly synthesized the political and the personal, and an ardent pride in race.

Their common race apart, America could hardly provide a greater contrast than the lives of these two young Americans. Even in Birmingham, Angela had been somewhat protected from the drawbacks of being black, and thereafter she had, at least superficially, enjoyed the life of a favored daughter of the affluent West. George Jackson, born and brought up in Chicago, then Los Angeles, had had nothing to enjoy: not fun, not money, not education, not honors; and principally not freedom. He was a living expression of intolerable injustice. And yet, by their strikingly different roads, they had reached the same destination: convinced Marxists, they were certain that the only hope for a just America lay in revolution.

Their politics made them equals. So did their intelligence. One of the more amazing facts of our time is that the eleven years' imprisonment to which society condemned George Jackson for the seventy-dollar robbery that he may or may not have committed as a teen-ager failed to make him either subhuman or angry. Bitter he certainly was. "My credo is to seize the pig by the tusks and ride him till his neck breaks," he wrote to Angela. "I want something to remain, to torment his ass, to haunt him, to make him know in no uncertain terms that he did incur this nigger's sore disfavor." But as these very words show, it was a bitterness that could take time off for irony, for ridicule, a bitterness held under control. He was also prepared to use force. "We die too easily," he said more than once, wishing that resignation were a less marked feature of American blacks, wishing that the Black Panthers could be more like the Viet Cong, and blaming black mothers for the broken spirit of their sons. An early message to Angela was, "I hope that since your inclination is to teach you will give serious consideration to redeeming this very next generation of black males by reaching for today's black female." But as well as bitter and determined, George Jackson was funny, charming, vibrant, immensely intelligent and clearheaded. And though he disclaimed being a writer, he wrote in his letters some of the most singing prose that contemporary America has produced. He was a triumph of human survival in inhuman conditions, an American Solzhenitsyn.

How did he survive—and not only survive, but develop, educate himself, even (though it seems odd to say it of a convict killed in prison) fulfill himself? Early in the years of his indeterminate sentence he discovered Marx, Lenin, Trotsky, *et al.*, and it was this intellectual discovery, plus a self-imposed daily routine of pushups, that preserved his self-respect. In growing excitement he mastered Marxist-Leninist theories of economics, revolutionary organization, the dialectic of history. Then he turned to the prophets of black guerrilla warfare—George Lewis, James Carr, W. C. Nolen, William Christmas. He studied Frantz Fanon and Che Guevara and Mao Tse-tung; and he read and read and read. Moreover, as far as was possible in prison conditions, he applied his lessons in practice. His aim was "to transform the black criminal mentality into a black revolutionary mentality," and he attempted this by behaving with unimpeachable integrity himself, so as to weld his fellow convicts into a front united against the authorities.

No wonder the authorities picked on him, and his fellow militants, Clutchette and Drumgo, when they needed first, second, and third murderers; and equally no wonder Angela fell in love with him. Here was a man whom she could respect, admire, respond to on intellectual, political, personal levels all at once; a man who incarnated the struggle; a man of her own people. She wrote:

> I have come to love you very deeply. . . .
> I have used these words very seldom
> in my twenty-six years—because I could not
> have meant them very often. . . .

and again:

> My memory fails me when I search
> in the past for an encounter with
> a human being as strong and
> beautiful as you. Something in you
> has managed to smash through
> the fortress I long ago erected around my soul. . . .

Much later, when George Jackson was dead, she declared that her friendship with him was "the most beautiful and most painful experience" of her life:

> There was something about him which no one could help loving. I think it was George's incredible capacity to love, himself. All the innocents he loved, and so each time he reached out to someone it was always with a gesture of love. It's funny how some people expect me to be jealous of the "love letters" he wrote to other women. I found them very beautiful—and, in a sense, that was part of what attracted me to him: his immediate affinity with all who had not committed themselves to the enemy ranks.

There was little chance, Regents or no, with or without a job, that Angela was going to quit her commitment to the Soledad Brothers. When the Regents finally fired her—having cautiously waited until June 19, when the university was shut—they used her speeches and especially those in defense of the Soledad Brothers to do it.

"Inflammatory," is what the Regents called four speeches Angela made during the academic year 1969–70.

So provoked were they by what was called "the improper nature" of Angela's remarks as a university professor that you would have thought she had placed tacks on their chairs instead of speaking words to some students. Dewitt Higgs, one of the Regents, referred pompously to a report of a policy decision by the American Association of University Professors as if it were the Word from Sinai. The 1964 AAUP ruling on its members' remarks outside the classroom "asserts the faculty member's right to speak or write as a citizen free from institutional censorship or discipline" but "calls attention to his special obligations rising from his position in the community: to be accurate, to exercise appropriate restraint, to show respect for the opinions of others and make every effort to indicate that he is not an institutional spokesman. . . ." It was evidence of the pretty pass things had got to when all this solemn semantic nonsense was needed to fire Angela who, it appeared, had "failed" to show "appropriate restraint." These were her additional sins: she had repeatedly demanded admission of Communist Party members to the faculty; she had claimed that academic freedom was meaningless unless it promoted political and social freedom; she had labeled the Board of Regents "unscrupulous demagogues running an outmoded institution." Finally, she had called for mass demonstrations in support of her ends and had spoken out in defense of the Soledad Brothers.

Angela's worst "crime" was semantic. She referred to the police as "pigs." She said the Regents "killed, brutalized, and murdered" the People's Park demonstrators at Berkeley. Her most "objectional words" came in a Santa Barbara speech in which she said "We should call things by their names. When people start saying that we are subversive, we should say, 'Hell yes, we are subversive; hell yes! And we are going to continue to be subversive until we have subverted this whole damn system.' "

Lurching ponderously to defend Angela's "intemperate"

speeches, the AAUP then presented the Board of Regents with an oddly roundabout, even rambling explanation: instead of simply observing that she wanted to reach a lot of people in their own language, and had every legal right to do so, they waxed philosophical in a statement that shone with three-dollar words:

> There is difficulty in penalizing Angela Davis for vituperation, name calling and bad taste in her polemics. . . . In this day and age when the decibel level of political debate . . . has reached the heights it has, it is unrealistic and disingenuous to demand as a condition of employment that the professor address political rallies in the muted cadences of scholarly exchanges. When Miss Davis in the classroom has shown herself entirely capable of thoughtful and soft-spoken discourse. . . . She explained her platform terminology by reference to her personal background and to the needs of communicating to her audiences a view of reality which inheres in the choice of style and would not be conveyed by "respectable" synonyms. When asked how she would judge if this style were used publicly by her own professors or her older colleagues, she replied that it would depend on whether it appeared as a natural expression of the person's background or as a false note, adopted only as a tactic.

They could merely have noted that for intemperate remarks Angela never held a candle to Spiro Agnew or Ronald Reagan.

Speaking in defense of the Soledad Brothers from the Federal Building steps in June, Angela received the news that she had been fired. She said, "What has happened to me is only a tiny, minute example of what is happening to them. I suppose I lost my job because of my political beliefs.

They can lose their lives. . . . Had I contrived to wage my own struggle without exposing the threads which tied it to the fight against political repression in the prisons, I could have been accused of the utmost hypocrisy." Jonathan Jackson stood beside her as she spoke.

A statement Angela had made the September before seemed even more valid in that June of 1970: "The Regents seem intent on meting out punishments which concur with the fascist tendencies of the times. . . . Let there be no doubt, my stand is forthright. As a black woman I am used to fighting and I will continue to fight now." And there was plenty left to fight. What few people realized was that Angela's case was still pending in the courts, that she could still be reinstated to her teaching position the following year (which, in January 1972, while in the Palo Alto jail, she was). In light of their intense interest in Angela it seems a fair assumption that the Board of Regents of the State of California knew very well indeed that the courts could still force them to rehire her. Perhaps they knew it all too well.

PART VI/SAN RAFAEL
AND AFTER

"People have said I am obsessed with my brother's case and the movement in general. A person that was close to me once said that my life was too wrapped up in my brother's case and that I wasn't cheerful enough for her. It's true. I don't laugh very much any more. I have but one question to ask all of you and the people that think like you: What would you do if it was your brother?"

—JONATHAN JACKSON

On August 7, 1970, Jonathan Jackson walked into a courtroom at the Marin County Civic Center where a San Quentin prisoner, James McClain, accused of having assaulted a guard, was on trial for his life. The prosecuting attorney was questioning a witness whose name was Ruchell Magee, another inmate at San Quentin. Jonathan Jackson took four guns from beneath his coat. According to one account, he then called, "All right, gentlemen. We're taking over." McClain, facing the jury said, "I have been unjustly accused. I want to be a free man and I will be!" Giving the impression that the event was anything but planned, Jackson, McClain, Magee, and another inmate witness, William Christmas, huddled together to confer on a plan. The four armed men took hostages: three jurors, Assistant District Attorney Gary Thomas, and Judge Harold Haley. McClain is said to have taped a sawed-off twelve-gauge shotgun to the judge's neck.

Within moments the whole group had moved out of the courtroom. There was a news photographer waiting in the hall. He was a friend of Judge Haley's, but at McClain's urging to "take all the pictures you want," the photographer produced the now famous pictures of that moment. The group got into an elevator, and descended to the ground floor of the building. Jonathan Jackson reportedly cried, "Free the Soledad Brothers by twelve-thirty," indicating a possible intention to exchange the hostages for the three Soledad Brothers.

Leaving the Hall of Justice, McClain, Jackson, and the others moved toward a parking lot, where they reached a rented yellow van. Putting the hostages in the rear, they climbed in and started the engine. Officers arrived and began milling about. The sheriff, unwilling to risk a shooting, gave an order that no weapons be fired. There were, however, a number of San Quentin guards, all trained to obey the strict rule of that jail: no inmates must ever be permitted to use hostages to secure freedom. John Matthews, one of the San Quentin guards, was near the van, armed with a rifle. As the van drove away, there was gunfire. Some say two shots were fired from the front of the van. Others say Matthews, in defiance of the sheriff's instructions, fired first. Whatever the sequence, once Matthews had opened up with his rifle, other guards joined in the violent barrage. The van stopped, the door opened. On juror had been shot in the arm; the assistant district attorney was badly wounded. McClain, Christmas, the judge, and Jonathan Jackson were all dead. No one had mentioned Angela Davis' name.

On August 11, 1970, a warrant was issued for Angela's arrest. She was charged—jointly with Ruchell Magee, the only convict who survived the San Rafael shooting—with murder, kidnapping, and conspiracy in the events of August 7. She was accused of having given the guns to Jonathan Jackson, and under California law anyone providing a weapon with the intent it be used for a crime is as guilty as whoever commits that crime. The indictment reads exactly as if Angela had pulled the trigger.

The "facts" on which to base a conspiracy charge were

that Angela knew and had worked with Jonathan Jackson and had visited San Quentin two days before the shootout. "Eyewitnesses" claimed to have seen her near the Marin County Hall of Justice just before the incident—some said days before, some said hours. Apart from this, there was very little evidence indeed. There were the guns, however. Yet they were legally purchased and owned: Angela was never accused of illegal possession of weapons. The state also noted that Angela had spoken out on behalf of the Soledad Brothers.

On August 16 Angela disappeared and on August 19, 1970, she became—a person with no criminal record whatsoever—the third woman ever to appear on the FBI's Ten Most Wanted list.

FBI agents arrested her on October 13, 1970, in a Howard Johnson's motel in New York. She was with a man named David Poindexter, who was arrested for harboring a criminal. He was subsequently acquitted. It was impossible to "prove" he had ever seen a newspaper, an FBI poster, a television broadcast, and therefore that he knew Angela Davis to be a wanted woman. As he left the courtroom newsmen asked him, "What are you going to do now, Mr. Poindexter?" He replied, "I am now going to do what I have done every evening of my adult life. Go home and read the papers and watch the newscasts on the television."

Meanwhile Angela was in prison. On arrest she had been taken in handcuffs by federal agents to the Women's House of Detention—the Greenwich Village jail she had so often seen and so often been frightened of in high school. To begin with, she was put in what she called, in an unpublished account of the experience, "an excuse for a psychiatric ward." "When all was quiet, I was led to a bare, nauseatingly yellow-walled six-by-five cell. I was stripped of everything, cigarettes and underwear included. I was alone in my cell with nothing but the outside demonstration chants ringing late into the night." In the weeks that followed she learned much about "jail-induced madness." Women were heavily drugged or treated like children. Officials harassed prisoners with insistence on petty details. Smoking was permitted only in the day room and getting a cigarette was an elaborate charade in which the women, forbidden to handle fire, waited on the whim of a matron with a match.

Prison culture was a surprise. Naïve in the ways of jail life, Angela made the other women smile. The first night they warned her to "Watch out for Mickey," who would try to get her that night: Mickey turned out to be the mice running loose in the cells. "In a sense our daily struggles with Mickey, the various means devised to get the better of him, were symbolic of a larger struggle with the system which was desperately attempting to destroy our humanity."

She learned, too, about "family life" inside a prison. "I was astounded to discover that so many of the women considered themselves to be gay (if only for the duration of their incarceration). The women organized themselves into families: mothers, fathers, daughters, even grandparents. Many of the homosexual relationships grew into 'marriages' and lasted into the future beyond jail walls.

"A few young sisters adopted me as their mother. I recall with especial fondness a young woman of sixteen with a very intense beauty about her who decided she would be my daughter. Housed with the adolescents, she always managed to persuade the officers to let her into my corridor. She had a way of saying, very quietly and lovingly, but also firmly that she just *had* to be with her mother. We were both very happy when she was finally released on bail, but neither of us could pull off a dry-eyed goodbye. . . . Another very beautiful young sister told me that if I were gay, she would marry me. She gave me what, in her eyes, was the supreme compliment."

Harriet, a prisoner with a very strong, dark, ageless face, made herself Angela's champion. Harriet "knew her way through all the crevices of the Women's House of Detention. Most of the officers would never cross her; they knew what the storm inside her could be like; they knew what havoc it could wreak. . . . At first I did not understand how it was that Harriet could visit me during my two-week solitary confinement. Even the matrons were prohibited from conversing with me. When she would approach the little cubicle, no officer ever dared to turn her away. She would come each day with little presents; you did not ask where she had obtained them. Always she would ask whether there was anything in the world I desired. I complained about having to use the toilet all out in the open and about having to dress exposed to the apartment windows across Sixth Avenue and exposed before the window of the door to my room. My protests to the officers had been futile: with Harriet things were different. Moments after I related my problem, she was back with all the paraphernalia needed to hang curtains around the toilets and to drape the windows of this improvised solitary cell.

"Harriet was eager to give all she had for her people, our people. . . . The jailors began to grow wary of the solidarity welding us all together."

It is clear from Angela's account that her two months in the Women's House of Detention were important not only to her, but to other prisoners—and apparently were to the prison staff. After she had been taken away one of the matrons sent her a letter (published in the anthology *If They Come in the Morning*):

> We miss you, gloom has settled over the jail,
> because our light and inspiration have gone. . . .

On October 14 Angela was arraigned and bound over for extradition to California. Haywood Burns, one of her lawyers in New York, says, "I met her face to face for the first time the day she was arrested. She is, if anything, stronger every time I see her. Her zeal, tempering her, comes out stronger and harder and sharper than ever. I think she's that way because she's a true revolutionary. She has principles she lives; she doesn't separate her ideas from her actions. She is no goddess, but she does approach the ideal in her ability to free herself of those things that might hinder you from business. Her business is to fight."

Two days before Christmas of 1970 Angela was awakened in the middle of the night and taken to the warden's office. She was informed she was being extradited to California. Permission to return to her cell for her belongings was refused. Handcuffed, she was taken to a van and, escorted by no fewer than ten squad cars, left New York at three in the morning for McGuire Air Force Base at Fort Dix, New Jersey. Claiming that they feared the hijacking of a commercial airliner, officials detailed a California Air National Guard plane to carry her to Marin County.

On January 4, 1971, she was arraigned, and from that time on her life consisted of long weeks of pre-trial motions in court and longer months of nights in the Marin County Courthouse Jail.

Once he had recovered from the wounds received on August 7, Ruchell Magee, the other accused, was taken back to San Quentin, where he had already spent seven years. Magee, a seventh-grade dropout from Louisiana, had been sent to jail for a 1963 Los Angeles robbery-kidnapping conviction resulting from a hassle over a ten-dollar marijuana deal. There were guns involved, although no one was hurt. Sentenced to one year to life, Magee had been fighting the conviction ever since. Charged with the murder of Judge Haley, Magee faced a death sentence, which, before capital punishment was abolished in California in 1972, was mandatory for a convict. An accomplished jailhouse lawyer (although prison records claim that his IQ was 78) Magee filed handwritten petitions in his own behalf and managed to get several judges removed from the case, tying it up for nearly six months. "He fights essentially alone, using only his painfully gathered knowledge of the legal system and the notoriety of the case to get his message out; that he is innocent because he was imprisoned illegally in the first place, that he has been kept a 'slave' for seven years and that what happened on August 7 was, in his words, a 'slave rebellion' to remove the conditions of his bondage," reported Sol Stern in the *New York Times*. Eventually Judge Richard Arnason severed the two cases: Ruchell Magee and Angela Davis were to be tried separately.

While pretrial motions were argued by Angela's lawyers —Howard Moore, Margaret Burnham (the young black woman who had been at school with Angela in Birmingham), and later Doris Walker and Leo Branton (who came in for the actual trial)—a vast political campaign was being mounted in Angela's defense.

Liberez Angela, Freiheit für Angela Davis the posters, buttons, pamphlets read all over the world. Much of the campaign's strength was due to the Communist Party of the U.S.A., but all kinds of people—liberals, radicals, church groups—sent money to pay committee members' and lawyers' salaries as well as other expenses. It wasn't only the Party that supported Angela, but thousands of others, each with his own reason. The soul singer Aretha Franklin offered to post Angela's bail early in 1971 (if it was granted), "Not because I believe in Communism but because she is a black woman and she wants freedom for black people."

Understandably enough, however, the people who worked hardest were the Davis family, who banded together to work for Angela. Now married, Fania Davis Jordan campaigned as far as Europe and the Soviet Union and stopped her travels only to give birth to a baby, Angela Aisa. Ben Davis spoke whenever he could take time off from his job as a running back with the Cleveland Browns. Reggie, in college, and Mr. Davis, with the gas station to run, could do less, but they too traveled to support the accelerating campaign. Mrs. Davis just canceled ordinary life. She had always feared that her daughter's radicalism would provoke a backlash. Now that this had happened, Mrs. Davis rose to the challenge, traveling to almost every state in the country, speaking at rallies everywhere, never stopping.

When she first heard that her daughter had been arrested, she wasn't sure she could take it. She thought, How will I manage? Will my heart just give out? But, she adds, it was Angela, her powers of survival and courage that cured everyone else's fears. The first time Mrs. Davis had ever been inside a jail was to visit Angela in the Women's House of Detention. The moment she saw her daughter smile, she knew it would be all right. Everyone went to see Angela, she says, hoping they could do something for her; everyone came away from jail feeling Angela had done something for them. Of Mrs. Davis, Haywood Burns said, "She's doing very well. She's very strong. It's all very new for Mrs. Sallye Davis. In fact, before all this, she was afraid to fly and Angela made her lose that fear. And I think Angela's going to make a lot of people lose a whole lot of fears. Her mother is bearing up regally under the whole thing."

The United States Government was also doing some quiet but busy campaigning. For some time, although news reports appeared only in March 1972, the United States Information Agency had been carefully explaining "to all audiences, especially influential opinion-molders, how the Anglo-American judicial processes differ, sometimes sharply, from the judicial processes in other countries." USIA officials were told to emphasize that Angela was "innocent until proven guilty; that the trial was open; that loose charges by the Angela Davis Committee of genocide against black militants were not justified by the facts. Ken Towery, the agency's policy chief explained, "As soon as this broke, I knew it would be a *cause célèbre* around the world—that's the way the Commies operate."

Month after month the pre-trial proceedings continued. Angela was granted her constitutional right to act as co-counsel in her own case. Chief Counsel Howard Moore and his colleagues argued motion after motion, often, it seemed, to deaf ears. Moore, a distinguished-looking man who has much charm and a way of gently deflating pretension, is an Atlantan who defended the Black Power leaders Rap Brown and Stokely Carmichael. He represented Julian Bond (his brother-in-law) in his successful battle to be seated in the Georgia legislature. His arguments that Angela could never receive a fair trial in Marin County, where the incidents of August 7 had occurred, were fiercely eloquent. In the hope of obtaining a fairer trial Moore asked that it be moved to San Francisco, an urban center with a racially mixed population. Finally, Judge Arnason granted the change of venue.

The trial, however, was moved not to San Francisco but to Santa Clara County. In Santa Clara there are two towns where a trial might be held: Palo Alto, the rich white suburban home of Stanford University; and San Jose, a small industrial city with a reputation for extreme conservatism and a population only 2 percent of which is black. Experts testified in court that prejudice in general and against Angela Davis in particular (now seeming to be a highly dangerous criminal, surrounded as she was by unprecedented security precautions) was even greater in San Jose than in Marin

County. But the trial was set to begin in San Jose on January 31, 1972.

Repeatedly denied bail, Angela was forgetting what freedom looked like. The probation authorities at San Rafael recommended bail; it was denied. The sheriff of Santa Clara County recommended bail; it was denied. In June of 1971 it was so sure that bail would be granted, so impossible in the circumstances that it be refused, that Mrs. Davis made her reservations for California. Her anticipations were smashed when Judge Arnason again refused the request.

On February 18, the Supreme Court of the State of California abolished capital punishment, and as a result on February 23 Angela was finally released on bail of $102,500. (Collateral was provided by the McAfee Family Cooperative, a vast dairy farm in the rich San Joaquin Valley run by Rodger McAfee, who calls himself a Communist; he said, "Promoting the issue of Angela Davis is the important thing in the world I could be doing right now.")

When Angela left the North County Courthouse that day, she called her release a "victory for the people" and vowed to "work for the release of all political prisoners." But under the terms of bail she was required to live in Santa Clara County and could not travel outside the Bay Area. Nor was she allowed to speak in public. Bail could always be revoked.

"I think," she said, "that most of all I'd just like to go around to the little black communities and meet the people and thank them. It's only because of what they've done that I got out on bail." Earl Caldwell of the *New York Times* wrote, "Right now she is learning about the outside all over again. Getting in and out of a car, she often holds her hands together as if she were still handcuffed."

Angela had spent sixteen months in jail.

"Prison invites sleep. It seems that the sparse alternatives of imprisoned existence inexorably push people into willful forgetfulness. Yet I have also seen in many women the most incredible triumphs over these forces."

—ANGELA DAVIS

Marin County Courthouse Jail, San Rafael, California, July 1971:

I am going to jail for the first time in my life—to see Angela. Leaving the elegant house where I am staying in Berkeley and where, at this morning hour, everyone still sleeps, I drive fast. The freeway is smooth, empty, the coffee, the radio music, the speeding car ease away anxieties as the fog rolls back across the mountains that protect San Francisco from the rest of America. The sky comes out sharp, blue, as I drive across the San Rafael bridge and pass San Quentin.

The freeway descends into a valley of cars—new, used, trade-ins, wash, fix—and rises up again into the lush green hills of Marin. The Civic Center is just below the freeway. Frank Lloyd Wright's fancy-free sensuous curves of pink concrete, gold spires, and blue plastic domes that match the California sky as faithfully as a reflection are cuddled by undulating green countryside. A splendid Byzantine motel with lawns more perfect than Astroturf and flowers that glisten from the fog-dew the night has left. August 7 has also left its residue. Barbed wire, guards in khaki, their sky-blue patches embroidered with yellow suns bulging on beefy arms, every glass door equipped with electronic devices.

As I pass under a checkpoint, a machine whines; I'm

ordered back by the guard, eyed coolly by a matron as I remove watch, earrings, and belt. Cleared. Inside the smell is of wood, polish, paneling, rich carved smells. The offices give off the elliptical corridors that curve round an open well, a Guggenheim Museum specially built for Marin County. The various departments, like booths in a street fair, lack only vendors yelling, "Pay your parking tickets here," "Welfare this way, come and get it." At the bottom of the well a whole green garden grows, fed by daylight through the plastic overhead. At the end of a morning's justice, with the prisoners despatched to their cells, officials, lawyers, and the press take the elevator to the rooftop cafeteria where fountains play and the sky shines and you can almost touch the hills.

The delicate attention to detail in the Civic Center has missed the jail. The waiting room is decaying, cigarette butts litter the floor on both sides of a plastic wall through which inmates and friends talk by telephone on visiting days. In their office at the far end two bulky guards drink coffee from paper cups. Signing in, I wait for Angela's lawyers.

The cubicles in front of me are divided by little wire fences. Two young lawyers arrive and are admitted to the cubicles from my side. Two boys are brought to the other half from somewhere deep inside the jail. Conferences are held; the lawyers depart. The two prisoners—one black and sturdy, the other white and thin—wait in their boxes. No one comes to take them away to the relative freedom of the jail beyond. They glance out at me, wanting only, it seems, a smile. They hammer on the wall, they shake at the doors. Still no one comes. The hammering stops and begins again, until—after minutes? hours?—a guard removes the young men.

After being searched by the matron—I'm glad she is not the dour-faced one with blue-black hair and squared-off shoulders who comes to court with Angela—I am passed through two solid metal doors. To the right there is a cell with a peephole. The matron bangs on it with her bundle of keys. As I enter the cell I see Angela.

Well, all I really see of her is the back end, bending over in a pair of red shorts and a tee shirt. Today she has been out to exercise. Too often she is kept alone inside— officials say she will teach other women karate if they let her mingle. Exercise, like everything else, becomes a privilege to be conferred and revoked at the apparently random will of officials. Angela straightens up, smiles widely, reaches warmly to hug me. Pulling on a sweater, she sits down. We sit around the large table littered with papers and books, Life Savers, chewing gum, and cigarettes. A few feet wide, a few feet longer, the cell contains an iron bunk bed packed solid with books. There is a rough metal shower, a toilet, and sink. The photograph of George Jackson, smiling broadly, warms the little room.

We talk for a long time. I pass on all the messages people have sent with me; we discuss the case, the trial, and her dislike, even her fear, of personality cults. It is both the political and the personal Angela talking: the two seem to have merged. "The point," she wrote, "is to discover the threads which tie a personality (which, at bottom is the creation of the media) to the needs and dreams of the masses."

There are jokes. Her capacity for enjoyment seems part of her general capacity to cope. There is a cool acceptance of reality. I'm amazed to find her so able to stand aloneness, to preserve a sense of self, even when it is not supported or rewarded by the outside world. Though facing a possible death sentence, she seems one of the sanest people I've ever met. Maybe because the intellectually well-endowed are the best equipped to withstand solitude? I don't know. At the very least Angela keeps busy. She has books, newspapers, even a radio. But there are no windows and you cannot walk out at will.

Marin County Courthouse Jail, San Rafael, November 1971:

The wind is fierce in San Rafael. It is Sunday and the Civic Center is closed for business. Wind slaps the building hard. I enter the jail accompanied by Margaret Burnham, one of Angela's lawyers. Elaine Brown of the Black Panthers is visiting too, and she tells very funny stories and everyone laughs a lot.

Angela, quieter this time, is more determined than ever to survive and to win. The photo of George Jackson still hangs in the cell. But he is dead now, murdered in August. There is pain in Angela's eyes at the mention of him.

She discredits rumors that her eyes are bad, that she has glaucoma, that she has suffered pain from her teeth. Instead she tells about the chiropractor. She had had pains in her neck and back; the doctor came. While the matron watched in astonishment, the doctor suddenly picked Angela up, tossed her on the floor, and began a therapeutic stomp on her back. Picking her up again, he tossed her in the air.

Despite the laughter, she is not optimistic, not at all. Soon she will be moved to Palo Alto. "They'll probably come in the middle of the night again, like they did in New York. When do you think it will be?" she asks Margaret Burnham. But she will not be sorry to leave Marin, where "the concrete possibilities open to the few women are all but nonexistent."

For these women, as she recorded in an unpublished manuscript, life is a progression of inanities. There is television, a few trashy books, tiny scraps of notepaper. A decent pencil is hard to find. There are children's games and "whether we are seventeen or seventy, as prisoners we are always 'girls' to them." The women's day room has something the men's lacks: washing machines, clothes dryers, ironing boards. "Women, because they are women, presumably lack an essential dimension of their existence if they are separated from their domestic chores. . . . When, out of boredom, more than can be accommodated actually want to do the work, it is the black women who are ignored . . . if no one feels naturally drawn to this work, it is, of course, the black women who are ordered to do it.

"Sleep emerges as a kind of luxury just because it involves unconsciousness, the absolute negation of an already empty existence. Matrons use the bed to tease and taunt inmates to 'good conduct,' just as they give and take away favors and privileges continually flaunted."

Each time Angela goes to court she is taken through the tunnel that leads directly from her cell. A group of men await her on the other side of the electric door and "when they really feel like seriously flaunting their authority, they wait until we are in the elevator descending to the prisoners' tunnel and will flatulently, but in all seriousness, unsnap their gun holsters—all a show for my eyes only."

Palo Alto County Jail, January 1972:

It is three days before Angela's twenty-eighth birthday, her second birthday in jail. I know Palo Alto well, having spent a year in this lush suburb at Stanford University. I hated this town then, with its expensive lawns and flowers and sunshine that kept people busily isolated from one another pulling weeds. This time the town rearranges itself in my eyes through a protective filter of newfound and well-liked friends. I even knew this Civic Center: I used to pay my parking tickets here.

"Humane, as jails go," Howard Moore tells me. The searching is cursory, the matron admits she does not like it, and escorts me to the cell. It consists of a narrow corridor with three minuscule cubicles. There is a desk littered with papers, a huge electric typewriter, hundreds of cards from foreign countries. One cubicle has an iron bunk bed and a sink, the second a toilet. The third is Angela's "sitting room" with a portable TV, a radio, an enormous bright banner embroidered with her name and the colors of liberation—black, red, and green. Books everywhere—Wilhelm Reich, Marcuse, Kate Millet, legal books, Marx, law books, articles in German and French, and half-written pages and pages of yellow paper. An ashtray piled with the pipes Angela has taken up to cut down her four-pack-a-day habit. A thermos of coffee.

Howard Moore settles into a corner with a book. Angela sits crosslegged beside him wearing a green print smock, brown ribbed tights and sweater. She is very thin and very pale and tired. The cell is chill with the damp cold of concrete floors and walls. Later the heat comes on, rising until it becomes suffocating, nauseating. We begin to talk and the hours pass and it grows hotter. She picks at the supper tray a matron brings, her conversation still focused on women in jail. Howard Moore and I try more idle talk, and for a moment all of us chat about travel. She looks wistful for a moment, but not very. Illusions for her are few and dispensed with quickly. But again she turns to prisoners, talking softly, intensely, about aversion therapy, about the brain-damaging drugs that make inmates more docile than cabbages. There is no fear in her voice, only urgent concern.

As I get up to leave, stretching the cramps from my muscles, she looks for a letter from the ten-year-old boy who sent her his five-dollar Christmas money. It is nearly eight —I have been there for six hours. I say "take care" and she smiles and Howard and I leave together. Angela stays behind, looking very alone.

Outside it is raining, the sky wet and black, and I get in the car to drive back to a warm house full of friends and light. The image of her in that jail, burdened with her dreadful knowledge of what they do to prisoners, alone but sure, stays with me.

17/THE PEOPLE VS. THE STATE OF CALIFORNIA

"If I am convicted, I will see the jurors as having been willing or unwilling accomplices in a conspiracy presented by the
state. If, on the other hand, I am not convicted, I'll see that
as a victory of the people."

—ANGELA DAVIS

Judge Arnason called case #52613, *People of the State
of California vs. Angela Y. Davis,* to trial at 10:20 A.M. on
February 27, 1972. The tiny courtroom in San Jose was isolated in the back corner of the building. There was room for
only fifty-nine members of the press and the public. Eight-
foot-high fences surrounded the courthouse, and every person entering was subjected to a thorough search and a scanning by two metal-detecting devices.

A panel of a hundred and sixteen prospective jurors
was called, and by March 15 an all-white jury composed of
eight women and four men was seated. Angela expressed
her "confidence in the women and men presently sitting in
the box."

On March 27, while the prosecution's opening statement
was being delivered, the remaining two Soledad Brothers,
John Clutchette and Fleeta Drumgo, were cleared in San
Francisco of charges in the case linked to that of Angela
Davis.

Assistant Attorney General Albert Harris outlined the
prosecution's case against Angela Davis. Driven by her intense love for George Jackson, she had helped organize the
plot, bought the guns, and supplied the money for the shooting at San Rafael. She had acted from passion, "A passion

that knew no bounds, had no limits and no respect for life
. . . not even the life of George Jackson's younger brother."
She considered herself married to George Jackson and she
used her only face-to-face meeting with him on July 8, 1971,
in a holding cell at San Quentin for a "close passionate and
physical" involvement. "Her basic motivation was not to
free political prisoners but to free the one prisoner that she
loved—George Jackson."

On March 29, 1972, Angela Davis, acting as co-counsel,
rose to deliver the opening statement for the defense.

It was a skillfully organized, articulate, rational statement, untainted by histrionics, that asked the jury to consider the poverty of the case against the defendant and
coolly set out the defendant's rebuttal. It was, more than
anything else, a legal masterpiece. For Angela meant to win
this particular round, and if the only means to do so was
American legal strategy, well, she would prove a first-class
strategist.

With an air of total confidence that the People of California would give her justice, she declared that she had indeed campaigned for the Soledad Brothers—and for other
political prisoners—openly, legally, as it was her right to do.
It was a proof of innocence, not guilt. She declared she was
a radical, long involved in the liberation struggle of minority
groups, in the campaign against the Vietnam War, in the
fight to raise the status of women, in the defense of academic
freedom. "In all my activities," she said, "my goal has been
to aid in the creation of a movement encompassing millions
of people, indeed the majority of the people in the United
States today, a movement which will ultimately usher in a
more humane, socialist society."

Yes, she had bought guns—in her own name and giving
her own address. And for the best of reasons: there had been

"hundreds and thousands" of threats on her life. "We who were working toward radical social transformations felt that it would be necessary to obtain means to protect ourselves."

Yes, she had known and liked Jonathan Jackson, but that didn't mean she had conspired with him to commit an act that she thought prompted by despair.

Yes, she had gone to ground when a statewide search for her was announced. "I had ample reason to fear unjust treatment by the courts of California. . . . I had reason to fear the prospect of many months of incarceration without bail, an eventual trial before an all-white jury, therefore not a jury composed of my peers, and many other obstacles to my efforts to protect my innocence."

She faced head-on the subject of her feelings for George Jackson. The prosecution would have the jurors believe "I am not the person you see standing before you, but rather an evil, sinister creature pushed to the brink of disaster by ungovernable emotions and passions." The truth was, much as she had longed for his and other political prisoners' freedom, she had worked for it only in open, lawful ways. And she paid her tribute to the prisoner who had died in captivity: "My love and affection for George grew. However, it was not until I had been arrested and had become, like him, a political prisoner that my relationship with him grew stronger and my affection deeper."

Angela had never wanted to be a cause. But when destiny decreed otherwise, she resigned herself. Nor had she ever wanted to be a public performer, but this fate too she had learned to cope with. After the enormous pressures of the past three years; after the sensationalism, and the vilification and the threats on her life; after the beginning and the tragic ending of her friendship with George Jackson; after the deadening long months in three different jails—she arrived with all her intelligence, humor, and humanity intact, to conduct her successful defense at San Jose.

Perhaps she survived it so well because she has grown accustomed to being on trial. From September 19, 1969, when she was dismissed from her post at UCLA, she had been continually answering one accusation or another, permanently subject to a greater or lesser degree of public curiosity. While she developed new skills to meet the demands made on her, she undoubtedly also grew new skins behind which her true personality could remain undamaged. Perhaps the very acceleration of events over the last years was a crash course in the toughness that she needed. More probably her whole life had been a preparation for the events of 1972—from the childhood on Dynamite Hill, through a youth spent quietly expanding her intellectual horizons, to the discovery of the socialist politics and the full public identification with and commitment to the struggle of her people which, in the courtroom, she so proudly claimed her own.

When on June 4, 1972, she was acquitted of all charges by a jury in San Jose, she announced her determination to commit her life to freeing political prisoners, and to prison reform. She was free at last. But others were not. Not yet.

EPILOGUE: MORE NOTES ON A JOURNEY

Most of us need someone to help us break out of the acceptance world. Angela is that someone for me. Though I had known, of course, about American injustice and racism and repression, it was she who made these issues real.

So, because events beyond our control deposited us at the same time in the same school, I have come, ten years later, to learn a lot about those obscure corners of American society into which standard liberals like myself rarely bother to look. Only in tracing her journey did I reach the point in mine where I saw that the good will of liberal New Yorkers could be tarnished by subtle racism. Only in reviewing the attacks against her at UCLA did I realize that in America the black Communist bogeyman is bigger than the white Communist bogeyman. Her story has taught me one important truth (among others): America nurtures her best—but with specific goals in mind for them; if they do not accept, they can be punished, disinherited, cut off without a cent in the going currency.

If Angela has not yet made a radical of me, she has unmade me a liberal. It won't be so easy now to produce the old automatic responses. Henry James was right: it is a complex fate to be an American. The last time I saw Angela before she went to jail was on a fine spring day at UCLA. The sun shone over the bright-green campus, students settled onto the grass to share their lunches and their laughter as the rally for the Soledad Brothers began. They grew quiet as Angela rose to speak. She was very tall, very straight, and she looked at us, talking to us and about us, as she read:

"They came for the Panthers and I was not a Panther
so I did nothing.
And then they came for black people and I was not
    black
so I did nothing.
And they came for the Chicanos and I was not a
    Chicano
so I did nothing.
And they came for the radicals and I was not a radical
so I did nothing.
And then they came for me. And there was nobody left
    to help me."

Angela's biggest impact on me, however, is not as an instructor on social issues, but as a person. I like her, I find her kind and funny. And I admire her enormously. She is the most committed person I have ever known. She lives her life according to what she believes. She has achieved the goal she set for herself: to merge the personal and the political to the point where they can no longer be separate. Despite the trials she has faced, the emotional and physical pain she has suffered, she has not become embittered, nor rigid in her politics, but has remained a person capable of great depth and warmth of feeling.

People see her as a black leader and as a liberated woman. There is something else that matters to me: she is an American. American-born and -bred, American-educated and -privileged, her life is committed to improving her country and its people.

A friend in the Middle East sent me a letter not long ago. He found the words I was looking for: "She amazes me in a grateful kind of way. The woman gives me an acute inferiority complex with her self-possession and calm. Long Live."

INDEX

Index

Academic freedom, 11, 157, 160, 173, 196

Adorno, Theodor, 103, 111, 112, 115, 117

Advance, 70–71, 73

Agnew, Spiro, 174

Alexander, Deacon, 131, 132, 133

Alexander, Franklin, 131–132

Alexander, Kendra, 131, 132

American Association of University Professors, 173, 174

American Friends Southern Negro Student Committee, 36, 51

Aptheker, Bettina, 69, 70

Aptheker, Herbert, 69–70

Arnason, Richard, 185, 187, 188

Baldwin, James, 85, 125

Bank of America, 166

Bardot, Brigitte, 115

Bengis, Ingrid, 33, 73, 75, 77–78, 81, 82, 83–84

Berkeley Free Speech Movement, 70, 123, 124

Birmingham, Alabama, xv, 17–24, 25, 32

Black, Howard, 87–88, 89, 90, 91

Black Bourgeoisie, The (Frazier), 33

Black Panther Party for Self-Defense, 132

Black Panther Political Party, 132

Black Panthers, 11, 47, 66, 99, 118, 142, 143, 160, 166, 170, 192, 200

Blackburn, Robin, 119

Bond, Horace Mann, 25

Bond, Julian, 187

Boy Scouts, 30

Brandeis University, 73–84, 97, 102

Branton, L., 45, 185

Brewster, Kingman, 166

Brooklyn, New York, 52–56

Brooklyn Heights Youth Center, 67

Brown, Elaine, 192

Brown, Rap, 187

Burnham, Louis, 45

Burnham, Margaret, 45, 70, 185, 192

Burns, Haywood, 8, 25, 38, 39, 186

Butor, Michel, 90

Caldwell, Earl, 188

California, 120–130

California, University of, 123, 138, 141–175
  dismissal of Angela Davis, xi, 6, 11, 145, 146, 157, 165–175
Carmichael, Stokely, 118–119, 120, 130, 132, 136, 187
Che Lumumba Club, 131, 133, 134–135
Christmas, William, 171, 179, 180
Clark, Gregory, 132
Cleaver, Eldridge, 6, 147, 153, 155
Cleaver, Kathleen, 13
Clemenz, Manfred, 81, 82, 88–89, 92, 104
Clutchette, John, 168, 171, 195
Committee for a Sane Nuclear Policy, 69
Communism, Black, 39–41
Communist Party, xi, 5, 9, 11, 39–40, 42–44, 45–46, 70, 115, 116, 130, 131–138, 143, 145, 147, 148, 150, 157, 158, 161, 173, 185
Congress of Racial Equality (CORE), 39
Congress on the Dialectics of Liberation (London), 117–118
Connor, Eugene ("Bull"), 19, 20, 21, 45
Cooke, Alistair, 7
Crisis of the Negro Intellectual, The (Cruse), 39
Cruse, Harold, 39
Cuba, 147
Cuban Revolution, 79–80, 91

Daily Bruin, 138, 142
Davis, Angela:
  arrest of, 181
  attitude toward opposite sex, 81–82
  bail, 188
  birthplace and date, 17
  California and, 73–74, 120–130
  childhood, 17–37
  Communist Party membership, xi, 5, 130, 131–138
  conversations in jail, 189–194
  Cuban experience, 147
  defense campaign, 185–187
  disappearance of, 181
  dismissal from University of California, xi, 6, 11, 145, 146, 157, 165–175
  education, 29, 36, 51–84
  extradition to California, 183–184
  Frankfurt years, 104–119
  Girl Scout activities, 30–31
  interest in philosophy, 80, 90, 97–103, 111–112
  Paris days, 79, 85–93
  personality, xiv
  political development of, 45
  pretrial proceedings, 184, 185
  prison days, 181–188, 189–194
  religion and, 30
  San Rafael incident and, xii, 8, 10, 12, 179
  Soledad Brothers defense campaign and, 167–175, 181, 196, 199
  trial of, 9–10, 187, 195–198

UCLA and, 138, 141–175
warrant for arrest of, 180
Davis, Angela Aisa (niece), 27
Davis, B. Frank (father), 19,
22, 24, 26, 27–28, 30, 36,
37, 39, 45–46, 48, 74,
120, 186
Davis, Ben (brother), 17, 19,
22, 25, 27, 28, 29, 31, 32,
51–52, 186
Davis, Fania (sister), 5, 17, 19,
20, 25, 28, 29, 30, 31, 32,
34, 47, 121, 129, 169, 186
Davis, Frank M., 40
Davis, Reggie (brother), 17, 21,
25, 29, 37, 186
Davis, Mrs. Sallye (mother),
17–18, 19, 20, 23–24, 26–
30, 31, 32–33, 34, 36–37,
39, 40, 45–48, 56, 70, 74,
82, 120, 137, 186, 188
"Discovery of What It Means
To Be an American"
(Baldwin), 125
Divale, William Tulio, 142–
143, 144
Douglass, Frederick, 38
Drumgo, Fleeta, 167, 168, 171,
195
DuBois, W. E. B., 38, 70
Duras, Marguerite, 90
Dutschke, Rudi, xvi, 114

Elisabeth Irwin High School
(New York City), 56, 59–
72
Eros and Civilization (Mar-
cuse), 101, 124
Express, L', 9

Fanon, Frantz, 141, 171
Federal Bureau of Investigation
(FBI), xi, 6, 12, 80, 142,
143, 144, 150, 181
Fisk University, 36
Frankfurt, Germany, 102, 104–
119
Franklin, Aretha, 185
Frazier, W. Franklin, 25, 33,
34–36, 39, 40
Freedom Riders, 21, 71
Fried, Erich, 106, 111, 115
Fromm, Erich, 103

Galamison, Milton, 72
Genet, Jean, 99–100, 155
German Socialist Students'
League, 105
Ginsburg, Allen, 76
Girl Scouts, 30
Glass, Sidney, 129
Goldberg, Lannie, 77–78, 81,
82
Greenwich Village, 57–59, 181
Guevara, Che, 171
Gullen, Nicolas, 155

Haley, Harold, 179, 184
Hare, Nathan, 6
Harris, Albert, 195
Hegel, Georg, 111
Heidegger, Martin, 100
Hemphill, Paul, 17, 21
Herndon, Angelo, 41–44
Herdon, Leo, 42
Hieber, Elfie, 105, 106, 107–
108, 109, 136–137
Higgs, Dewitt, 173
Hitch, Charles, 150, 165–166
Hoffman, Abbie, 7, 75

Hoover, J. Edgar, 7, 59
Horkeimer, Max, 103, 118
Hughes, Langston, 48

If They Come in the Morning,
    183
Institute for Social Research,
    102, 111–112
International Youth Festival of
    Peace and Friendship
    (Helsinki), 80

Jackson, George, 28, 165, 168,
    169–172, 191, 192, 195–
    196, 197
Jackson, Georgia, 169
Jackson, James, 45
Jackson, Jonathan, xii, 169,
    175, 179–181
Jackson, Penny, 169
Jackson State University, stu-
    dents killed at, 166
James, Henry, 199
Johnson, Lyndon, 143
Jones, LeRoi, 6
Jordan, Angela Librée, 186
Jordan, Fania Davis, 186
Jordan, Jane, 86

Kalish, Donald, 138, 143–144,
    145–146, 150, 154, 156
Kant, Immanuel, 99, 106, 111,
    112–113, 124
Keniston, Kenneth, 119
Kennedy, John, assassination of,
    91
Kent State, students killed at,
    166
King, Martin Luther, 21, 23,
    38, 39, 91, 160

Kovel, Joel, quoted, 3
Krahl, Hans Jurgen, 105–106,
    110
Kunstler, William, 9

Laing, R. D., 119
Lamotte, Madame, 85, 86–87,
    92
Lewis, George, 171
Life, 7
Long, Reverend, 30, 36, 46
Los Angeles Peace Council, 143
Lowell, Robert, 76
Lucy, Autherine, 23
Lynn, Eddie, 127

Magee, Ruchell, xii, 179, 180,
    184–185
Makeba, Miriam, 119
Malcolm X, 14, 83
Malle, Louis, 115
Mao Tse-tung, 171
Marcuse, Herbert, 97–103, 104,
    111, 114, 115, 116, 120,
    121, 123, 124, 127, 130,
    133, 134, 136, 147, 161
Marin County Courthouse Jail,
    184, 189–193
Marx, Karl, 111
Mason, Flo, 67
Matthews, John, 180
McAfee, Rodger, 188
McAfee Family Cooperative,
    188
McClain, James, 179–180
McGee, Henry, 163
Melish, Billy, 52
Melish, Dennis, 52
Melish, John, 52
Melish, Rev. John, 53–54

Melish, William Howard, 51–56, 74, 82
Melish, Mrs. William Howard, 52, 54, 56, 64, 67, 68
Melish family, 36, 51–56, 69, 74, 91
Menne, Lothar, 116, 118, 119
Michael X., 119
Miller, O. G., 167
Mills, John, 167–168
Mitchell, Charlene, 131
Mitscherlich, Alexander, 109
Mitscherlich, Tommy, 105, 107, 109
Montgomery, Ed, 142–144, 147, 150
Moore, Howard, 185, 187, 193, 194
Moreau, Jeanne, 115
Morgan, Neil, 123
Mount Holyoke College, 74

National Association for the Advancement of Colored People (NAACP), 38, 69, 71
National Council of American-Soviet Friendship, 53, 54
Negt, Oskar, 112–113
New York City, 31–32, 51–72
New York Times, 7, 10
New York University, 27, 31
Newsweek, 7, 9
Newton, Huey, 132
Nixon, Richard, 39, 166
Nolen, W. C., 171

Oglesby, Carl, 102, 116
Ohnesorg, Beno, 117
Oliver, C. Herbert, 45

One-Dimensional Man (Marcuse), 101

Pacht, Jerome, 151
Palo Alto County Jail, 193–194
Paris, France, 79, 85–93
Poindexter, David, 181
Politics of Experience, The (Laing), 119
Pollock, Frederick, 103
Pozzvoli, Claudio, 107–108, 110, 117
Pretrial publicity, 10
Prosser, Gabrielle, 38

Rafferty, Max, 8, 159
Reagan, Ronald, 8, 11, 120, 123, 159, 174
Reston, James, 18
Robbe-Grillet, Alain, 90, 98–99
Robinson, Paul, 100

Sachs, Murray, 76–77
San Diego, California, 122–130
San Francisco Examiner, 142
Sarnoff, Irving, 143
Saxon, Mr., 149
School Desegregation Act (1954), 23
Scottsboro Boys, 44, 45
Seale, Bobby, 155, 160
Seeger, Pete, 72, 116
Sevareid, Eric, 7
Shores, Arthur, 23
Shuttlesworth, Fred, 56
Shuttlesworth, Mrs. Fred, 56
Singleton, Robert, 13, 131, 132, 153, 154–155, 163–164
Socialism, 38, 48, 115, 134

Soledad Brothers, xi, 145, 167–175, 179–180, 181, 195, 196, 199
Southern Christian Leadership Conference (SCLC), 39, 46
Southern Conference Education Fund, 55
Southern Negro Youth Congress, 39, 45
Sozialistischer Deutscher Studentenbund (SDS), 105, 115, 116
Springer, Axel, 117
Stagg, Christy, 86
Stein, Gertrude, 35
Steinbrink, Meyer, 54
Stepinac, Aloysius, 53
Stern, Der, 9
Stern, Sol, 185
Student Non-violent Coordinating Committee (SNCC), 131, 132
Students for a Democratic Society, 11, 66

Tennessee Coal and Iron Railroad Co., 42
Thomas, Gary, 179
Times Square, rally in, 69
Towery, Ken, 187
Trinity Episcopal Church (Brooklyn), 53–54
Turner, Nat, 38

United Front Against Fascism, 146
United Negro College Fund, 35
United States Information Agency, 186
US, 132

Vietnam War, 113–114, 196
Village Voice, 9, 81
Viva Maria, 115

Walker, Doris, 185
Wallace, George, 21
Waltham, Massachusetts, 73, 74
Walton, Sydney, 6
Washington, Booker T., 35
Weathermen, 66, 75
Wells, Warren Wesley, 44–45
Wesley, Cynthia, 24
Wittenberg, David, 105, 114, 116
Women's House of Detention (New York City), 58–59, 181–183, 186
Women's liberation, 132, 160
Woolworth's, 57, 68, 69
Wright, Charles, 9

"You Can't Kill the Working Class" (Herndon), 41
Young, Charles, 151, 165, 166

Advocates
P. O. Box 155
Hot Sulphur Springs. CO 80451-0155